NO LONGER REQUIRED

BY

Bill Linskey

Pisces Press

British Library Cataloguing-in-Publication data

A catalogue record for this book is available through the British
Library.
ISBN 0 9537285 0 1
First published in 1999 by Pisces Press.

Enquiries should be addressed to the author
c/o Pisces Press,
Suite 162, 95 Wilton Road.
London SW1V 1BZ.

E-mail. lifeboats1042999@aol.com
Fax no   0207 630 8124

Dedication

To the dead and living seamen of the Merchant Navy during World War Two. And to the men of the Royal Navy, without whose protection there would have been many more dead, and fewer living merchant seamen to thank them.

To fellow survivors from the Arctic Convoys, especially those shipmates in the North Russia Club.

To every seaman, regardless of nationality, who can still remember the sound of depth charges, torpedoes, bombs and every other missile aimed at them.

Most of all, to the firemen and trimmers who shovelled all those tonnes of coal and laughed as they swore that it was their last trip.

We got there, and the lucky ones are still here.

I was quite unable to get these seamen across oceans without them swearing.

Thanks to Pat Shaughnessy for his good memory, to my wife and amanuensis Eunice, who listened and wrote. Also to Robert Pendleton for suggesting the book should be written and then having the patience to edit it. To Vincent and Willa Rea for their encouragement.

Photographs courtesy Vincent & Willa Rea,
Jarrow. Tyne and Wear.

Cover design by Fran Gutteling, Battersea.

Poem by Alfred Benjamin, of Newfoundland.
Canadian able seaman deceased 1941

Cartoon by Philip Zec.
Copyright Mirror Syndication International

Printed and bound by
Brook Green Print. London W14 OPR.

CONTENTS

Part One : **From Jarrow to the Ships**
1921 - 1939

Part Two: **War in the Atlantic**
1939 --- 1942

Part Three : **The Frozen North Archangel, Russia**
1942 --- 1943

Untitled. By Alfred Benjamin of Newfoundland.

You have seen him on the street,
Rolling round on groggy feet;
You've despised him when he's been out on a spree,
But you didn't see the trip on the dark and lonely ship
through a submarine and mine-infested sea.

You have cheered the Navy lads
On their heavy Ironclads;
You can spare a cheer for Tommy Atkins too.
You may have a touch of funk
When you read "BIG MAIL BOAT SUNK"
Did you think about the Merchant Service crew?

You have mourned about the cost of every vessel lost
It put you in a pessimistic mood.
But you have never said, "Well done!"
Or congratulated one
Who helps to bring your wife and kiddies food.

He has brought your wounded home
Through a mine infested zone;
He has ferried all the troops to France by night.
He belongs to no Brigade,
Is neglected, underpaid.
Yet is often in the thickest of the fight.

He has fought the lurking Hun
With an ancient four inch gun,
And he does his bit to get them on the run.
Yet you've never heard him boast,
To the folk who need him most.
In fact, he's sort of reticent and glum.

Wouldn't you feel that way, too
If, no matter what you do,
You're still another Merchant Service bum?
He can collar Huns and smite 'em
To the real "ad infinitum";
And for Wops he doesn't care a damn.
His social standing's nil,
You regard him as a pill
But you've got to hand it to him — he's a man!

Prologue

'I've had one ambition from the time this war began: to find a German soldier, surrender to him, and spend the rest of the time in a POW camp.'

I said this to Joe Beck on the deck of the SS Ashby, outward bound for West Africa to pick up iron ore. The sun was shining, the sea blue and apparently benevolent.

'That's a worthy want,' he agreed, 'I might join you. They're out there under the water looking for us. When they find us they'll blow us up and if we're lucky we'll be able to swim like the clappers and surrender.'

He was absolutely right. They were out there in their little sub and within the next hour they torpedoed our ship. They didn't wait for me to surrender; they buggered off. Joe couldn't have joined me; he was dead.

The twenty-eight of us who survived in the lifeboat saw torsos, limbs and heads floating in red water. The sharks came soon but the Germans had long gone.

The bodies disappeared quickly too.

PART ONE:
FROM JARROW TO THE SHIPS:
1921-1939

Chapter 1
Jarrow – A Little Ireland.

I was at an ex-seaman's funeral when I began to reflect on how many Merchant Mariners had died in recent years. I thought I would try to tell about life below decks in the coal-burning steamships before I too fell off the twig and failed to leave a record of these very common seamen. This is the story of my war in the Merchant Marine. It is almost sixty years since it began.

I wouldn't have been there if I hadn't joined up long before the war in Jarrow, County Durham; the place prepared me for the hardship, the hunger and the sheer absurdity of life in the Merchant Marine. We lived in 'Little Ireland' as though our grandparents had brought Connemara over on their shoulders. The majority of the population was Roman Catholic, even the few English. There were dozens of mean streets of terraced houses built for English miners. But the mines in Jarrow had closed decades earlier and now Irish shipyard workers filled them.

The main Irish streets, Albion, Stanley, Princess and Cambrian Streets more or less comprised the boundaries of 'Little Ireland'. Besides the dwelling houses, these streets had numerous *Common Lodging* Houses.These cost from sixpence to ninepence a night and so were crowded with itinerant Irish workers.

A common night sight in this poverty stricken area was the moonlight flit - when wheelbarrows carrying a few sticks of furniture were wheeled to another area to escape paying overdue rent.

Once you entered these houses you were in Ireland. There was always an old woman--aunt, grandma, God knows who she was, everyone had one. She would be dressed in black, seated at the fireplace. On the wall hung religious statues of the Virgin or a picture of the Sacred Heart although I don't remember even the very religious ever going to church. The cooking was done on a coal fire with food kept warm on a hob. If it was a bad week the kids were sent to the shop to buy any bruised fruit and vegetables. They were really cheap.

The legacy of hatred and pain of a subjugated people had crossed over with them. The old aunt or grandmother could be relied on to feed Irish history into the next generation. We learned of the Potato Famine, the Black and Tans, the most hated Oliver Cromwell and Orangemen, as well as the treacherous men who allowed the English to keep six counties of 'our' island.

Aunt Nellie Nee lived in Albion Street. She was a political animal and she knew every dirty act committed by the English and Scots back to William of Orange. She also adored cowboy books and used their language in her everyday speech. Of anyone she disliked she'd say, 'I'll see him buried on Boot Hill.' She would write to her sons that she would 'put on her spurs and saddle the hoss,' meaning that she would go out to mail the letter.

Her grandson, John Nee, my cousin, was four years younger than I was. I remember him asking, 'Granny, are you a cow-girl?'

'Yes, I am me darlin,' and I've got four cow sons to prove it.' Shivers would run down our spines when they told us the old stories of the 'wee folk,' and the 'ghosties.' We heard of the black dog that was really the Devil.

He was called Fifty-Fifty and when he bit people they died and went to Hell. My Aunt Mary Anne lived in Alfred Street and was lucky enough to have a ghost as a neighbour.

The front door of Mary Anne's house was always locked, because Uncle Geordie kept his market stock in the front room. Sometimes I was able to sneak in and steal a small bar of chocolate.

We had to come in through the back door. They were very left wing and the room held a stack of communist hammer and sickle flags, as well as a number of banners essential for the demonstrations they attended.

Before I was born, Matty Storey had committed suicide in his back room upstairs. This was across the back lane from Aunt Mary Anne's back room. It was alleged that every year, on the anniversary of his death, his ghost would materialise and repeat the action of tying the rope around his neck and hanging himself.

In winter with early darkness I used to be terrified because I had to pass right in front of Matty's back door. I used to keep my eyes down and run just in case I looked up at his window and caught his eye.

Spectacle-wise, from her back window, Mary Anne had the equivalent of seats for the Football Cup Final; during the previous week she would invite a favoured few to drinks, scotch preferred, whilst they waited for the action at midnight. I was allowed to stay up one time and I glued my eyes to the window. I thought myself safe with all these well bevied grown-ups around me.

'There he is, there,' one of the men shouted. 'Where?' I couldn't see anything.

All the women were saying 'Ah, poor Matty, bless him,' and crossing themselves. I was quite upset. 'I didn't see him,' I said.

One old duck said, 'Oh well the Good Lord didn't want to upset you, you being so young. But he was there.'

What a mug, I believed it for years. The custom was laid to rest with the slum clearance about 1938. The house was demolished and poor Matty had to move I suppose. I never heard whether he went to the new housing estate with his friends. Some of his audience had themselves dispersed to the cemetery by then, perhaps they were making their own visitations somewhere.

The poverty was real. A man on the dole got 17 shillings a week (0.85 p) and 1 shilling (0.5p) for each child. When they ran out of dole time they went on the relief, commonly called the Pineapple, which gave even less money and a few food coupons. If a woman's husband died or left her, the only place to go, if she had children, was the workhouse, where they would do all the laundry for the local hospital in return for their beds and food. This food was mainly thin porridge, bread, potatoes and a watery stew.

Monday was wash day. You couldn't mistake it, because the thump, thump of hundreds of poss sticks beating the dirt out of clothes, made the whole town reverberate.

Pawnbrokers' shops proliferated. Women would meet in the street. 'I'm just taking His jacket and vest to the pawn.' Round they went to the pawnshop with the only decent garments the poor bastard possessed. These would spend the week 'in the pawn' and if the money on Friday stretched to it, the garments would be redeemed for the weekend. She would have got maybe one shilling and eight pence (0.8p) for them and had to repay one and eleven (0.9p).

Every year we school kids were given a pair of boots. The authorities knew they wouldn't be on our feet if they could be sold or pawned, so they punched a triangle of three holes in them to ensure they couldn't be sold as new. My Da became expert at filling in these holes and our boots would sit in the 'pawn' for weeks at a time. He must have paid the interest on one pair to keep them from being sold. When he finally redeemed them, my feet had grown two sizes and I couldn't squeeze into them.

Hopper's was the favourite pawnshop. He was an elderly Jew whom I now recognise as a philanthropist, if not a saint. If there was nothing of value in the house, desperate women would tie any old rubbish into a rag. This they held together with a knot or safety pin and the resulting parcel was called a 'wrap up.' They would take this bundle to Mr. Hopper, who would never open it, but respectfully ticket, and put it away. The pledger would gladly accept the sixpence or so that he would offer. The moment there was money; she would retrieve this pathetic bundle so that the whole system didn't collapse. Mr Hopper must have realised what was inside these wrap-ups. His method saved many a family from starvation.

Mr. Hopper couldn't save the entire community, however. In 1936, a consortium closed the shipyard, which left thousands without work and penniless. The shops shut because no one had any money to buy anything, so the town became derelict. Every corner collected groups of unemployed men, who were constantly moved on by the police for 'Obstruction.'

A large group of men walked to London to protest to parliament about these conditions; this was the famous Jarrow March. I'm not sure if it achieved anything, but at least it brought the place to the attention of the world. It always gets a repeat run whenever there is a documentary about poverty.

Besides the Jarrow March, Jarrow is also remembered as being the home of The Venerable Bede (673-735), the historian and educator. I went to the schools named after him, but alas, he didn't bring a lot of learning to me. I cannot recall ever being given any kind of test or exam but all the same I was put into the 'C' stream. The discipline was fierce. We accepted that if we got out of line we would be punished, first at school and very likely again on our return home. We knew the rules and we respected them; if we didn't we'd have hell beaten out of us.

We learned to read and write very quickly, however, because reading was the only entertainment. The local library was our Mecca, because it had a large selection of adventure stories. There was also a second-hand bookshop where we could buy Boys' Adventure Stories, Wizard, The Rover, Hotspur and Gem. We passed them to our friends and discussed the stories before trading them in for more of the same ilk. One of the serial stories in Hotspur was about an Indian Boy, a Maharajah, who went to public school, Eton or Harrow. At first, because his skin was dark he wasn't accepted and was given 'a jolly rough time by the other boys.' However, when they discovered that he was an all-round wonderful sportsman--at cricket, rowing and even boxing--they decided he was a 'Good Egg.' To this day I can remember the bemusement of us snotty-nosed, half-starved, dirty little boys. We doubted that such a world existed but the language used was a constant source of fun. For days after the latest issue we had enormous pleasure in saying, 'Oh, jolly good shot, Fothergill Junior' and 'well-played, Holyoak-Smith.'

Being in the C stream, I had several disadvantaged boys with me. One was Silas Tomlinson, who had what was known as 'St. Vitus' Dance.' We liked Silas, though, because he could joke about his condition. When he told jokes and pulled faces, we didn't know if he was having a fit or putting on an act. I suspect the teachers didn't either, because he got away with murder. When writing class was starting, I was unfortunate enough to sit next to him. He was always moving about, waving his hands, and making strange 'ugh ugh' noises loudly. Sometimes during a spasm, he used to stab the air with his pen. Lovely blobs of ink would fly around and the happy neighbouring recipients of this treasure would delight in it. They had an excuse for the mess on their books, as well as on hands, clothes, and hair. Our mothers couldn't scold us under the circumstances. We would have accused them of being cruel to Silas.

Oddly enough--like the Maharajah--Silas was a very talented athlete. Lacking boats and cricket pitches, he leaned towards somersaults and football. He could run like the wind; we were proud of him, because he could beat the upper classes in races. Unhappily he died when he was about 20 years old, though. He was a 'Good Egg.'

We were all from rough Irish families, but one of our pupils was a real misfit. Little Pat was from a large family, all with blonde hair and blue eyes, but he was prettier than any of his sisters. His voice was that of the most feminine girl. Nevertheless, he was totally accepted by us tough kids, he belonged to our Irish community and if necessary we protected him. That happened on St Patrick's Day when we played a silly game. Each of kids made himself a Bomb-Baiter. It sounds ominous but consisted only of a tightly rolled newspaper about the size of a turnip, tied by string with a string handle. We would ask each other, 'Are you 'I,' 'E,' or 'S'?' If the reply was 'S' (Scot) the Irish boy would whack the opponent. If 'E' (English) he'd be whacked harder. And of course the 'I's escaped as long as they didn't meet an 'S' or 'E.' Pat loved this game, but one of us always stayed near him, just for his safety.

I also remember Pat at Christmas. Before we broke up for the holidays we enjoyed a little school party, where they gave us an apple, an orange, and a couple of cakes. The cakes were irresistible to small hungry boys, so they went rapidly, but the orange and apple went home to our mothers to be shared with the family. We had to take our own teacup. Our teachers chose the most talented boys to entertain us. Some would do a little step-dance, and others would sing a song. However pedestrian the performances, they were greeted with rapturous applause.

Year after year, little Pat got up to do his party piece, his prim, squeaky, soprano voice ringing proudly:

Looking through the window, peeping through the lock,

Are all the children in their bed? It's past eight o'clock.

I too had a little poem, although I never had the courage to get up among these near professionals.

I had a little pony, his name was Dapple Grey,

I lent him to a lady, who rode a mile away.

Raised Voice:

She whipped him and she lashed him and she rode him through the mire, I would not lend my pony now, no matter who would hire.

I feel sure that if I'd had the courage to perform, I would have had a standing ovation.

Sadly, I was never called.

Anyway little Pat was another Good Egg.

On reflection I can honestly say that there was no bullying in our school—of Pat or anyone. We had several disabled boys, and there were also lads of Italian, African, Greek, and Chinese parentage We only expressed our dislike of Protestants, but they were at other schools and we could avoid them. During my schooldays I only met one Protestant, Charlie Cook, who had to be as poor as we were, otherwise his family wouldn't have been living in that Irish enclave. So on those terms he must have decided like many before him, 'If you can't beat 'em, join 'em.' We accepted him totally as 'one of ours.'

During the General Strike of 1926 there was no money and almost no food. Some of the enterprising men, such as my father, went to the hills and railway lines where the wagons loaded coal.

They would dig up the coal dust and put it into sacks. Then in the backyard they would mix the dust with soapy water and candle grease, mould them into what were called Duff balls and leave them to dry out before putting them onto the fire. They gave out furnace heat and in this way we survived.

Many didn't. At about this time my father was forever at wakes. My brother Austin, my sister Sheila and I would stand at the top of our street watching the funerals go by, very often of one of our relations. The Great War, tuberculosis and malnutrition all took their toll. Wounded ex-soldiers, many on crutches, would follow the corteges.

The horses were very important community members. Not only did they pull the funeral hearses, they also were responsible for the fire brigade's arrival at fires. As they didn't vary their pace, and the funeral speed was their preference, almost every place that went on fire burnt to the ground. I was told that they were the horse power for the ambulance. If true, it must have been of great benefit to have a lingering illness. You wouldn't stand much chance with a heart attack.

In 1928 when I was seven my mother died and my world shattered. She had cancer of the womb and had been ill for a long time but was in bed only for about three weeks. Until then I hadn't realised she had anything wrong with her. She was one of fourteen children, eleven of whom survived--six boys and five girls. Her eldest sister Mary Anne had run off to Gretna Green to marry-anything rather than slave after her six brothers-so my mother had stayed at home to help her mother in the house until she met my father at the age of thirty-four. While they were walking out her own mother became ill and tried to make her promise she wouldn't marry but would continue to look after the beloved boys. My mum must have said the equivalent of 'Sod that.' The priest also tried to bring pressure to bear telling her it was her duty but she insisted on her right to marry.

We three children would not have been as much work as her brothers and sisters but the financial pressure was worse. All her brothers had been working in the shipyard, so a lot of money for those days had come into the house. After marriage she had to manage on one pay packet.

I remember her as always being serious. I once asked her why, and she said 'because I'm worried, son.' I was the youngest and until she died I'd had lots of cuddles. They came to an abrupt end and I was told I had to be a little man and not cry. To this day I can remember the bleakness I felt and breathing in great gulps to prevent crying. I really wanted to go and huddle up in a corner and scream my pain and loss to the world. I was a little man instead because I didn't want to be the object of anyone's pity.

I remember my mother's face only from an old sepia photograph but the memory of her warmth is clear.

My father made the effort then to spend more time with us so I got to know him better. When he was sixteen he had joined the army under the assumed name of James Cumisk. He had fought in the Boer War and received medals. A strong athletic man, he became a PT instructor until he punched an officer and was court-martialled. He forfeited his medals, received two years' imprisonment and was discharged with ignominy. His cousin, my Aunt Nellie Nee, said it served him right for joining the bloody British Army. She was only glad he'd used an alias and hadn't sullied our Irish reputation.

He was a jovial man. We thought he was wonderful with all the acrobatics he could do; he was also a very good step-dancer. He went busking with Fluter Joyce and Johnny Melia, who played the accordion. Da took his dancing board and they went to all the surrounding towns and pit villages. The pit village people were always very generous and they would return with a capful of small coins. We'd never seen so much money in our lives.

However, my father drank more since my mother's death so there was less money. Even today, though, Sheila and I laugh about one of our worst homes, a terraced house next to a coal depot, which had a stable for horses. Unfortunately our house was next to the stable and the horses were just a wall away from us. We could hear them snorting. This wouldn't have mattered except two of them were temperamental and used to throw a tantrum almost every night. We would be asleep then suddenly woken by a sound like thunder. One or both horses would lash out, kicking their back legs at the wall, which was the wall of our bedroom. The wall would scream for mercy and the whole house shuddered under the impact. I got accustomed to the noise but Da never did, especially after a few drinks.

My brother Austin was seven years older than me then came my sister Sheila, five years older. My father did his best; he got us up in the morning, made sure we washed and generally saw to our needs. We used to be woken by 'the knocker-up,' a woman whose job was to wake up the men for their various shifts. If you lived in an upstairs floor she knocked on the window with a clothes prop.

Austin's first job was in 'the pit.' He hated it and didn't last long; even my father didn't blame him for that. A year or so later when he was fifteen, Austin heard of a Government plan to populate the Colonies and signed up to migrate to Canada. He was sent to a logging camp in Ontario. In the beginning he wrote telling us of a really hard life, with very hard men, but gradually the letters died off.

That was the last time I saw my brother until 1954 when a very different person returned.

When my sister talks of the same time it's as though we lived in different countries, different worlds, certainly different families. She speaks of big roasts on Sundays with lots of pudding, lovely stews, etc. I didn't see or eat them. When I ask her how we could have such different memories, she dismisses me with female scorn.

'You were always with your mates down at the docks looking at boats. I was on the scrounge, I often went at mealtime to Auntie Nellie Nee to pouch. I used to help her peel potatoes, then she'd ask me to stay to dinner.'

Nellie was my father's cousin and always had food because she had four sons who all had either war pensions or jobs. The youngest, named Austin like my brother, went to sea and was my hero. He would come ashore after a long trip, sun-tanned, sleek and seemingly as wealthy as the King.

It was from him I first got the fateful notion to join the Merchant Service when I grew up.

Chapter 2
Adventure

When I was twelve, a lad called Tommy Melia was my best friend. We would go and watch the ships, dreaming of the day when we would be able to go away on one. We would go to Tyne Dock where the timber vessels from Scandinavia docked. The Blue Star Line ships were refrigerated meat carriers; outward bound they would carry coal as cargo and ballast. They'd run to Argentina, Australia, New Zealand and the West Coast of the U. S. A. and Canada where they loaded meat and general cargo. The crew would come back looking like healthy Gods. That's what I wanted to be. Rich and well fed too. On the other side of the river at North Shields was a long concrete quay called the Staithe, where steamships loaded their coal for the next trip.

I little knew then how much of it I would be shovelling in the future.

Tommy and I roamed around constantly looking for adventure. Eventually we turned fourteen and could leave school to earn a living. It wouldn't be in ships yet because the joining age was sixteen and then only for cabin boys or galley boys, neither of which we fancied. I was tall for my age; the average height for a grown male was about 5'6' and I had already reached that some years before. Although I was certain I'd been starving for fourteen years, I'd inherited my father's strong, large-boned frame. I had dark hair and blue eyes, typical Irish I suppose. I thought I was pretty good-looking. I loved to sing, and joke and people thought me good-natured. Although sometimes things were tough I always had the feeling that something good would happen. Either today or tomorrow, anyway soon. Come to think of it – I still feel the same. I travel in hope, as the cliché goes.

As Tommy and I couldn't go to sea yet, we decided that we must have some sort of adventure. There was nothing in Jarrow but the Labour Exchange had loads of vacancies for young lads to learn trades so we enrolled to go to the Black Country to work in a foundry in Wednesbury. We were given a warrant to travel and another to get a new suit, as well as a work outfit which consisted of a boiler suit, a couple of shirts, a pair of heavy boots and a little case to carry them in. We also got TWO SHILLINGS each in our pockets. Neither of us had ever had a full outfit of clothes in our short lives and we felt like millionaires. We were fourteen-year old adults, leaving home. We were off on our Big Adventure.

What excitement! Neither of us had ever been on a train before. We spent the entire 180-mile journey with our eyes glued to the scenery. There was a brief break when we discovered that there was actually an indoor lavatory and a lever to flush water. A funny sign said something about not passing water while in a station. We didn't understand this but right now the wonders of the world were passing before our eyes.

The passengers all talked funny but they were nice and gave us a sandwich, fruit and sweets. One man asked us where we came from.

'Jarrow, County Durham,' I replied proudly.

'Ah yes, Geordies.' He nodded his head and smiled.

'What do you mean?' I was ready to be offended.

'That's what people from the Newcastle area are called.'

I must have looked doubtful.

'Different areas of England have different accents,' he explained, 'So they're called by nicknames Londoners are Cockneys, Liverpool people are called Scousers.'

In 1935 people had the dialect of the place they were born in and only seamen and strangers had ever heard any other. There was little radio and no television. Actors have told me that Geordie is the hardest English dialect to learn; when it's called for directors scour the profession for Geordie actors to play the roles, which is easier than anyone trying to master it. On top of this, we also had Irish accents and must have been well nigh incomprehensible to strangers. We too had never heard any other accent than our own, so we thought everyone was speaking a different language.

It was a Friday when we arrived. A welfare man met us at the station; he took us to our lodgings and then straight to the foundry, which was awful. The men were hot, dirty and sweaty and the noise was incredible. They told us our duties but I could neither hear nor understand. Every time we spoke they laughed at us, then called friends over to listen 'to these kids talk.'

We were mortified. We didn't look at each other until we were taken back to the lodgings and left alone.

'That was terrible,' said Tommy.

'It was the jaws of Hell,' I agreed. 'Did you see the devils with horns and pitchforks when you looked in the furnace?'

'Indeed I did, but I think they worked there,' said Tommy. 'I'm buggered if I'm going back.'

I agreed. We were quiet for a while.

'What do you think?' Tommy asked.

'I think we should go to London,' I said firmly. 'Sheila is there and your sister Bella. They'll help us get jobs.'

The Welfare man had given us ten bob each for weekend expenses. 'We haven't got enough money for our fares,' Tommy objected.

'We'll walk, it's only a couple of hundred miles.'

'I suppose that's okay,' he said, although his face told a different story.

We packed our small suitcases that night and hid them in the shrubbery at dawn. At breakfast we ate like gannets and filled our pockets with bread before leaving. Two fourteen year olds, dressed in our suits with our hair slicked back, we started on our trek with a pound between us.

Tommy started laughing. 'I was thinking of the landlady's face when she saw us eat this morning. I bet she'll be glad when she finds out we've scarpered.'

We walked as far as Birmingham—about 20 miles--and already we were knackered. We went to the railway station to look at the possibilities of hopping a train. It was easy. One at a time we waited until the ticket collector was otherwise occupied and walked past him. We didn't see any more on the journey and we arrived at Euston Station. I can't remember how we got past at that end.

London had always been our real destination, the Capital of the World as far as we knew. It was too late to find either of our sisters so we slept rough on the station. It was the first skipper we had done, but it certainly wasn't the last.

We had heard that all visiting Jarrow people met each other at King's Cross which is nearby. We had no money left and we hoped someone could tell us where Sheila lived. No one we knew was there but the police were. They asked us who we were, where were we from, how old were we, how much money did we have and what did we think we were doing? Then they took us to Albany

Street Police Station and tried to contact Sheila but she'd changed her job and address. Tommy had no better luck with Bella.

The police said they would send us to a place where we would be safe. We were in need of care and protection. They would let our parents know we were okay. We had a meal in the canteen, and then we were taken to Stamford House, a remand home in Shepherd's Bush. This brought us down to earth and we were really scared, although the police were quite kind.

We slept in dormitories, where all the boys were between ten and fifteen years old. Our own clothes were taken and we were given a blue sailor-type jersey and bell-bottom trousers to wear. 'Jersey, trousers, shirt, pants, vest, socks' was the mantra told us by the jailer, the order in which our clothes had to go into the flat basket that held them. Folded just so. Tommy and I repeated that phrase every time we met throughout our lives.

Our fear receded after a couple of days because we had food and a bed. All we worried about was how long we'd be left there. Our mornings and afternoons were filled with lessons and PT. The evening meal was at 6:00 PM, after which we had an hour for reading. Bed at 7:00 PM, then lights out immediately. There wasn't a lavatory in the dormitory, so that was it until 6:00 am. My bladder then must have been a better version than the one that I have now. At 6.00 a.m., we had half an hour PT- then lessons.

Bella came to rescue Tommy after about four days and put him straight onto a train home. They didn't find Sheila so Da had to come down. He had no money and it took him a few days to borrow enough for a one-way fare, so I was there for about ten days feeling very lonely and afraid I might never be rescued. The Court authorities gave Da the money for the fares home and a few bob to eat with. I expected a belting, but he didn't punish me. I suppose he remembered telling me of his own ill-spent youth.

But now I'd caught the travel bug and within four or five weeks I started working on permission for another trip. Da said I could try again if the Labour Exchange would help me but Tommy's Ma said he couldn't go under any circumstances. I went along to the Exchange alone and told the Supervisor that I wanted to work again; I'd like to go to London because my sister was there working at the Great Northern Hospital in Holloway Road. He said they would give me another chance but I must not let them down this time. With crossed fingers I promised. As an outfit went with each placement, I was issued with another suit, shoes, work outfit, underwear and small suitcase.

A Newcastle boy came with me to lodgings in Islington. We shared a nice clean room and had our meals provided. The food was basic but it was a great improvement on my previous irregular diet and it was plentiful. There was plenty of work with very poor pay for young lads. I saw a wanted notice outside a small foundry. The foreman was from Sunderland, a fellow Geordie who was as pleased as Punch to have another compatriot to commune with. There was a string of other Geordies working there and he took me under his wing, where I had to assume an interest in the Sunderland football team that had hitherto escaped me.

The job was great even though I was the general dogsbody. Any messages to be run were my responsibility, which got me out and around London. But although I was thoroughly enjoying my life, the dreaded wanderlust struck again when I turned fifteen. I gave in my notice, said good bye to my friends at work and started the 130-mile hike to Nottingham with only one ride on a motor bike. The labour exchange sent me for a job at a telephone factory, where I worked as a driller. It was mindless, repetitive boredom but I didn't mind. I was managing to save some money for my next move. The social Welfare Officer took me to a local Boy's Club, where they had billiards and tennis tables, but I didn't want to socialise. I thought they were strange boys who talked funny. He tried to get me into the football team but I refused that also so he gave up. I was absolutely alone. I walked out the soles of a pair of shoes. Boots the Chemist had a main library so I read a lot and went to the movies.

This self-inflicted solitude made me feel miserably lonely so when I'd saved enough money I made my way back to Jarrow. This time I travelled by local buses, sometimes I could go ten miles, sometimes twenty to the next big town. After about a week I arrived home. Da gave me a casual hug of welcome, as though I'd just been staying with an aunt for a week or so. Tommy was really pleased and I had to give a full report of what had been happening to me. 'I'm going the next time even if I have to run away from home,' he promised.

We were both sixteen in February. Neither of us could get work in Jarrow and my father was still unemployed. Tommy and I kept up our wandering round the town, down to the docks to see the ships. They were as exciting as ever but there were few jobs for boys and a lot of competition.

Da got fed up with being unemployed. 'I'm going to London, son, you reckon there's so much work there. Your Aunt Nellie said you could live with her until I save your fare. I'll send for you.'

After a couple of months he sent me the one-way ticket money. Of course I was ready to go within five minutes but Tommy had to sell his Mam the idea.

'Bill's going to London tomorrow and I want to go with him to live with him and his da,' he announced.

'Does Mr Linskey know?' She asked suspiciously.

'Oh, yes,' we assured her.

'All right, then.' She gave him the fare money and a few shillings. The next day she packed up sandwiches and an apple each for us and we were equipped for the 280-mile ride.

My da met us at the station. 'What's he doing here?' He asked, indicating Tommy.

'He's coming to live with us,' I announced happily.

Da raised his eyes to the sky. 'Jesus Christ.' However, he took us to his large room that had a double bed. Tommy slept on the settee. We all got work, Da in the building trade while Tommy and I took jobs in restaurants because we got meals and pay each day. We were pantry-boys, dishwashers or table-cleaners. The chefs all seemed to possess murderous temperaments. I liked to stay out in the restaurant after seeing a waitress being chased around a slippery kitchen by a cook wielding a knife. If we didn't like the food in one place we'd go somewhere else. Naturally we didn't always work together but if I left one place Tommy, knowing of the vacancy, would perhaps go there the next day.

All the London women we met called us 'Love,' 'Duck,' or 'Darling.' Cockney dialect still sounded odd. Everyone was called Pet on Tyneside. One time we were working in a place where the chef was an Italian who spoke Cockney with a villainous Italian accent. He was quite excitable. I was cleaning tables and Tommy was shouting orders up a dumb waiter to the kitchen above.

A waitress told Tommy her order. 'One roast, two soups, one fry up. Oh, and one apple, Duck.'

He yelled, 'One roast, two soups, one fry up and one apple duck.'

For a moment there was a puzzled silence. 'Howzat, howzat? Wotta you say?'

Louder Tommy cried 'One roast, two soups, one fry up and one apple duck.'

The reply started low and reasonable. 'Wosser matta you? I gotta da roast, da spaghetti, da bacon, da egg, da soup.' The voice gained volume. 'An I gotta da chicken, da chop, da ice-cream. But I no gotta da Apple Duck' At screaming pitch. 'I ain't gotta no fuckin' Apple Duck!!!'

The customers were screaming with laughter and the cockneys all yelled 'That's right cook, you give him hell!' Tommy looked around in terror at this madhouse, flung his apron to the floor and ran out into the road. I collected his pay for him but neither of us dared return the next day.

One day I finished my shift at 3.30 PM and strolled up Tottenham Court Road from the restaurant in Leicester Square. It was the middle of February 1938 and my seventeenth birthday would be in ten days, on 24th February. I was getting excited about it because after that, with a bit of luck, I'd be able to get work on a ship. I was dreamily window shopping, toying with the idea of a possible birthday present, and minding my own business when a well-dressed man approached me and flashed a card.

He first cautioned me with the words well known to all telly viewers. 'I'm a police officer. I'm arresting you for loitering with intent. I must warn you that you are not obliged to say anything but anything do you say will be taken down and may be used in evidence against you.'

I was flabbergasted. Was looking in shop windows illegal in London? I'd been taught to go to the police in times of trouble so couldn't believe that any policeman would arrest me for no reason. In my previous experience the police had been fair and kindly.

'What have I done wrong?'

He repeated, 'Loitering with intent to commit a felony.'

'I haven't done anything wrong.' I protested.

'That's what they all say. I'm taking you to the Station.'

He gripped my arm and took me across the road to the Tottenham Road Police Station. A police sergeant presided at a desk.

'I'm bringing this chap in on Sus (suspicion),' said the cop. 'At half past two I observed this man trying car doors, looking in cars and generally behaving suspiciously. I followed him for half an hour then I arrested him when he was trying to open a car door in Goodge Street.'

So I was charged and told to empty my pockets and sign for my property. They asked my age, address and who should be informed? Did I have anything to say?

'I haven't been in Goodge Street; I was on my way home from work. I was arrested in Tottenham Court Road.'

'Nothing to say,' said the sergeant. 'We'll inform your father.'

Because I was under seventeen I was put into a detention room with just a chair and table. I sat there absolutely shocked and frightened; I couldn't believe what was happening to me.

In a couple of hours the door opened and my Da appeared. It seemed like the Cavalry riding to the rescue. God bless him, my father never for a moment doubted my version. He had to sign a surety that I would appear at the required time at the Juvenile Court, Islington. To add insult to injury the date of my appearance would be my seventeenth birthday. If this was to be my introduction to manhood it didn't augur too well for the future.

When I appeared, they noticed my birth date and said I was no longer a Juvenile; so I was further remanded to appear in the Clerkenwell Police Court the following week. No one said 'Happy Birthday' of course. The delay only added to the worry but I swallowed my self-pity and continued to go to work. This would serve me well when I appeared in front of the Stipendiary Magistrate, who was a lawyer.

The detective was sworn in and gave his name, rank, etc. Then he read out from a notebook several pages of my alleged behaviour. He said that I had tried doors on cars.

'I followed him from 2.30 PM and I saw him try handles of cars in several streets. He stopped and looked in the windows of several more cars and in general behaved in a suspicious manner. So I arrested him in Goodge Street at 3pm.'

I was so angry I burst out, 'He's telling lies.'

The magistrate said, 'Be quiet, you'll get your chance to tell your side of the story later.'

After the detective had finished, the Magistrate said to me, 'Now you may question the officer.'

I thought, 'Bugger it, I'm not going to be railroaded by this lying bastard.'

'You claim it was in Goodge Street,' I began, 'But you arrested me in Tottenham Court Road, didn't you?'

'No, it was Goodge Street.'

'You say you arrested me at 2.56 PM?'

'That's correct.'

'And you had been following me for about twenty five minutes?'

He agreed.

'Funny that isn't it? I was still peeling potatoes until three o'clock. I signed off and went to the cashier for my day's wages at five past three. I've got the pay slip to prove it.'

He didn't speak but looked a little surprised.

'We arrived at the Police Station at quarter past three,' I went on. 'Why did it take so long to get there if you arrested me around the corner in Goodge Street?'

'It was the far end of Goodge Street.'

'Is that all?' asked the Magistrate.

'Yes.'

The detective left the box and they called another plainclothes man. I couldn't understand what he was doing there at first but I soon found out. He corroborated that he was on duty with the first detective and that they had seen me trying to open car doors and acting suspiciously.

Again I interrupted. 'I've never seen you before in my life! You weren't even there when I was arrested.' He looked embarrassed. The magistrate asked, 'Were you there when this man was arrested? Were you in the Police Station when he was charged?'

'Not exactly, Sir?'

'That is not an answer,' the magistrate said. 'Were you there?'

'No sir, I had to go away for a while. But I read the account in the detective's notebook and I believe it to be true.'

A barely audible voice in the gallery said, 'Lying bastard.'

The magistrate dismissed the second detective from the box and turned to me.

'You can either go on oath or make a statement from the box. Which do you want to do?'

'I want to go on oath.'

I was sworn in. I only got as far as collecting my pay before the Magistrate interrupted. 'That's enough, case dismissed.'

It was from this episode that my mistrust and dislike of cops were born.

No one in those days would believe that our gallant boys in blue would lie about kids to boost their arrest figures. I knew they did and that I was just lucky to get out of it. Probably if I'd had a previous record I could have started down a criminal path.

The whole episode had left a rotten taste soTommy and I decided to return to Jarrow and join the Merchant Service. I was old enough to go to sea as a cabin boy or a galley boy but I felt too grown up for that. I would raise my age to eighteen and join as a man, on full pay

Chapter 3
SS Albion Star.

The British Empire still covered vast areas of the world maps in red. Naturally such wide-flung interests required an enormous Merchant fleet to carry goods and an enormous Royal Navy to make sure that no interloper took liberties. Despite the massive number of ships, however, jobs were still difficult to get for firemen. I wanted to be a trimmer, an apprentice who wheelbarrows coal to the firemen working the furnaces. These were the lower orders in the Merchant Marine.

Any trip would take one new recruit so they would always have new blood. Nephews, sons, brothers or some lad recommended by a crewmember invariably snapped up these jobs. We had to rely on the alternative method--a pier-head jump. Ships sailed on tides, some of which would be at 11:00 PM or the early hours of the morning. These were the best for a jump because the vacancy depended on a seaman being too drunk to remember he was sailing or just drunk enough to say 'sod it.' If there were no ticket-bearing seamen around, the newcomer would be told by a mate to jump on board and he then trusted to luck that he wouldn't be thrown off again.

Tommy and I, not always together, would go around to labour exchanges looking for any work in the daytime. At night we would haunt the docks, hoping there would be a couple of firemen or trimmers who hadn't turned up. This went on for about three months and was quite exhausting. I began to think that I'd have to return to London when my luck changed. One night I was waiting at the docks with a bloke called Joe Christie, hoping to hear that some drunk hadn't shown up. Joe had done one trip before but hadn't been able to get a second. There were Jarrow fellows on board The Albion Star who were on our side. The opposition was three South Shields men who were also waiting to be called. South Shields and Jarrow folks were always rivals, why I don't know, but we kept it up in complete ignorance.

If the ship's crew was short and no one with a seaman's book was waiting, any able-bodied man would do. You didn't need a degree to shovel coal. These Shields men were older than Joe and me, though, so it didn't look promising. The Jarrow lads heard that two of the firemen were in the local jail and wouldn't be out in time. They had arrived, signed on slightly bevied and then decided 'bugger it, they wanted another drink.' They'd gone ashore, started a fight and got nicked.

'Just come on board and stowaway,' our mates said. 'Then at muster, Bill, you answer to the name of Ernie Molloy. Joe, you be Tony Rae. When we're out to sea, go to the Captain and give yourselves up. Tell him you want to work and give your proper names.'

It went like a dream.

The Albion Star sailed at 8:00 am. Going down the Channel, we were quiet as mice and after three hours we went to see the Captain, who was an ex-navy officer and wanted to be referred to as Commander Noakes. 'What can I do?' he said as he signed us on. 'I can't throw you overboard. I'll put you on articles.'

I gave my age as eighteen so I could work as a trimmer and get man's wages. The Second Engineer gave us our watches – mine was 16.00 to 20.00 hours and 04.00 to 08.00 hours. These two four-hour watches in twenty-four hours are called the 'Four to Eight.' I was pleased as Punch. Here I was, a seaman going to Madagascar in the Indian Ocean! For a three month trip, my only possessions the clothes I wore. At last life was starting.

I'd dreamed all my life about coming off a ship loaded with money. I don't believe I'd ever seriously thought about the work involved in getting that loot. The steam ships often carried coal as ballast, which they would sell at the destination port thus leaving loading space for the cargo we were to bring back to England. This would be meat collected in Madagascar so the Albion Star was refrigerated, which meant that the steam had to run the refrigeration as well as the ship.

We got a note to go to the slop chest (shop) to buy dungarees, undershirts and boots. The Chief Steward was a snotty bastard.

'Can I have short sleeved undershirts, please?'

'Nonsense, of course you can't. You'll be glad of long sleeves when you get down the stokehole.'

He was right.

At the start of every watch there was one furnace to be cleaned. The fireman pulled out all the clinkers—the stony residues from the burnt coal—to the deck, and the trimmer threw water on these until they cooled. You couldn't see for steam. Then the trimmer loaded the embers into the ash dumper and sent them up to the deck where the second trimmer threw them overboard. Both trimmers got coal from the bunker and brought it to the firemen until the watch finished. The whole process was repeated on the next watch. Both jobs were extremely hard, hot, and dirty.

My first watch started. We went midship to the 'fiddly-top,' a platform about twelve feet square made of iron bars. In the middle was a set of narrow iron rungs that led to a small platform about twelve feet down, where there were more rungs and another platform. This was repeated four times until we were in the stokehole in the bowels of the ship. The ash-dumper--a kind of dumb waiter--ran alongside the iron ladder. Its purpose was to take the clinkers and the ash to the deck for putting overboard.

The first watch wasn't too bad; it was all new and exciting. The coal was at the front of the bunker. After a week it became more difficult because the coal had receded and was harder to get at. Then the door was raised to man height so we could walk through it. The less accessible coal was shovelled into an iron barrow and tipped in front of the boiler.

I came off my first watch reasonably satisfied with my performance, except that I had blisters on my hands. I asked an old fireman what was the best thing to put on them.

'Piss on them, son. Piss on them.'

I did but it didn't help a lot, and over the next few days I was in agony. The blisters broke, bled and then formed again, repeating the process for at least a week until one day I realised that the skin had hardened and they'd gone.

This watch was also called the 'Black Pan' watch. The main meal was served to the crew at 5:00 pm, but the 'Four to Eight' watch was served after we bathed. We were given the food that had been left from the officers and the engineer's saloon, which was fabulous. I had grilled steak for the first time in my life, wonderful roasts, soups, green vegetables. Of course I'd eaten many of these things before, but of worse quality and certainly from worse cooks. I was in heaven except for my visits down to hell. Despite the hard work I was doing, I put on fifteen pounds during the whole trip and grew a couple of inches.

Still, about my first watch. After we finished I went with the others to the wash-house, where they each picked up a bucket. I was given a new one, marked to be mine for the trip, together with warm water and soap. They showed me how to clean myself with the sweat rag I'd used in the stokehole.

I told one of the men all I wanted to do apart from eat was go to my bunk He looked at me in horror. 'You can't turn in on the rake.'

'What's that?'

'Any dirty bastard who turns in without washing.'

This surprised me, although it shouldn't have. The miners from Jarrow were the cleanest people I knew and used a tin bath in front of the fire after every shift. I've seen a group of seamen point out a man who would turn in 'on the rake.' He merited the sort of disapproving face with pursed lips that women used to keep for an unmarried girl 'in the family way.'

After washing and eating I turned in. I was absolutely buggered from the ache of hitherto unused muscles. It seemed about five minutes before a rough hand shook me.

'Wake up, wake up, time to go down.'

'Wazzermatter?' I groaned blearily.

'Time to go down.'

'Down where?'

'To the stokehole you stupid prick.'

That woke me up. 'You've got the wrong man, I've been down once today.'

'What have we got here? Another fucking Jarrow Joker? Get bloody well up.'

By this time I saw that my fellow watch was climbing into their clothes, laughing like hell and the horrible realisation dawned that I had to go down again.

Shit.

I had an abscessed tooth, which was giving me hell. It blew up as we lay offshore at Port Said waiting for a pilot. It must have been the legacy of all the rich food I was devouring. The Chief Steward had to go ashore to arrange supplies with the Ship's Chandler so he took me with him in the row boat and dropped me at the dentist.

'Wait here, I'll pick you up when I've finished.'

I'd never been to a dentist and I was scared. I told myself I was now a man so I prepared myself to be stoical. The dentist gave me an injection and took out the offending tooth. He cleaned the remainder with what felt like a paint stripper and rasp. It was terrible, but like all horrors it finished. I felt a bit dopey from the injection but the toothache had stopped and I got quite chirpy.

All I saw of Port Said was from the dentist's window apart from what came to the ship in the bum boats. Dozens of them came filled with goods such as I'd never seen. I desperately wanted to buy something but had no money. Many of the crew were taking clothes up on deck to trade for something they coveted. As it was really hot, I didn't anticipate needing the one respectable jacket I owned so I took that. The goods were spread all over the deck, and every Arab was hawking his wares.

One asked a big fireman, 'Wanna buy a Rosary?'

He snorted his refusal then was sold a pack of 'feelthy pitchers' instead. A one-eyed Arab was very active; he was all over the place and seemed to have his finger in every sale. I didn't know what I wanted to buy but I wanted to be part of all the excitement. So I traded in the jacket. I will never know how I finished up in the focs'le holding a very large watermelon in my arms. I didn't need it with all the food we were given and I didn't like watermelon anyway.

I didn't say anything until one of the older firemen, Paddy Burns, told us in a puzzled voice, 'I've just sold two pairs of dungarees for these.' He threw down a small box of Turkish Delight. He was a hard tobacco chewing man. 'I must have gone mad.'

I felt a bit better. Then another threw down a pack of wooden clothes pegs. He didn't say a word. A couple of other old hands looked a bit sheepish but didn't speak. I suspected that they'd been taken too.

Paddy was brooding. 'I think we've all been hypnotised. Remember that one-eyed bastard? I bet it was him.' A bit of face saving brought general agreement that this was what had happened but one old seaman who had watched without trading or buying shook his head in disgust.

'What a crowd of useless bastards you are. It's bad enough being hypnotised but by a bloody one-eyed Arab? You shouldn't be allowed out alone.'

So we ate the watermelon and the Turkish Delight and looked at the pornography. It seemed to date from the sixteenth century and did nothing for anyone.

A couple of years ago I met Billy Morland who had also been a crew member. 'Do you remember being hypnotised on the Albion?' he asked.

I did of course but I was surprised that he had. What had started as a face saving story had grown into one of the merchant ship focs'le legends: 'Watch out for the one-eyed Arab hypnotist in Port Said.'

Up to this time all I had been able to do was work, eat and sleep, lurching tiredly from one activity to the next in a haze of exhaustion. Now I was beginning to take notice. We sailed through the Suez into the Red Sea. I was full of wonder at everything I saw; it seemed miraculous to have the shore almost close enough to touch. We saw just the heads of a train of camels, their arrogant faces looking at the passing ship.

If I had thought it hot before, I was to learn what an inferno is. To have crossed the Red Sea shovelling coal in a ship without air conditioning is to have been in Hell. Down in the stokehole the temperature was unbelievable, and the necessity to keep throwing coal to the firemen required a superhuman effort. We sweated buckets, we got the dreaded cramps, we got over them, then we cramped in another place. I hoped for a rapid death, as I believed my brains were cooking under my skull.

Coming down the ladder, we had to use rags because our hands would burn if we touched the rail. In the stokehole you'd be burnt if you touched a bulkhead. We couldn't wear gloves because we wouldn't be able to keep up the necessary speed. I was glad of my long-sleeved vest.

Anyone with a RC religious upbringing will know this hymn:
In Purgatory's cleansing fire, brief be my stay,
Help me to do thy will O Lord,
Just for today
And if today my span of life should ebb away
Help me to do thy Will O Lord,
Just for today.

I found myself singing this dreary little dirge with all the stokehole crew joining in. Prison cells and Purgatory seemed appropriate. I'd never had much belief in the fires of hell but here I was actually living in them. However, the watch always ended and we could escape at least to look at a lot of cool water in the ocean.

By the time Madagascar loomed on the horizon we were all shagged. We lay off a place called Bonne Mairie in the North. It wasn't what I'd expected. From the deck it looked green, very green indeed, but there was no sign of a town and I couldn't see a building of any description. It didn't have much glamour but I was too tired to think about it and I went to my bunk.

When I woke the scene was transformed. We were anchored out at sea and hordes of Madagascan stevedores were laboriously unloading our coal into giant buckets that held about a ton of coal. Our ship's winches loaded these buckets onto barges, which took them to shore. When the coal was unloaded, the holds could be cleaned ready for the meat cargo. It was a slow process. All I could hear of the stevedores' language sounded like *ariari* (which meant 'up') and *murra-murra* ('down'). When it was their mealtime they spread their food on the deck to eat.

Because we were at anchor, the fires didn't require as much hard labour. All we had to do was keep the refrigeration and ship's other requirements ticking over with the donkey boiler, which was only used in ports. We had to clean all the other boilers and rebuild a brick wall at the back of them, install new fire bars and scrape the smoke boxes, which each contained a couple of dozen seven-inch pipes.

This all took about a week, then we were able to go ashore. Behind the trees was a small village, which had rows of round mud huts with straw roofs going up to a point. It was like something out of the movies. And there was a meatpacking factory. The whole place stank of dead meat.

Alas, once you'd seen and marvelled at the native huts, there was bugger all else to see. The only recreation was a general store / canteen where we could buy a beer or a soft drink. Having jumped ship I hadn't brought a supply of books and there was little to read on board. I got a good tan but we were all bored witless. We were going to be six weeks in this dead hole.

The only break in the monotony was when my mate Joe Christie was taken to hospital. Perhaps he'd had a fall, I can't remember. I went to visit him. I took a clapped out old taxi the twenty or so miles to Majunga. Madagascar was a very poor French possession at the time and the fare was only a few coppers. Joe had a room on his own. He was a skinny tall fellow with a lugubrious face but it lit up at the sight of me.

'I'm bloody fed up, let's go to town.'

His clothes were in his room so he got dressed and we took a rickshaw to the centre. There wasn't a lot there either so after a while we went into a restaurant.The menu was lousy. I couldn't eat the food after the luxury grub we got on board, it looked like slop bucket refuse.

It was another two weeks before the meat was loaded. When Joe was back on board, we filled in time by walking around a lot and we saw quite a bit of the wild life. Many of the focs'le crew had been drinking heavily--which I'd not yet learned to do; they also went with the whores, a habit I never developed. Around this time, a strange contraption appeared by the side of one man's bunk, a round ball with a three-foot long tube at the end of it. There were two more the next day and then more until we had seven in all in the focs'le.

'What are they for?' I asked Paddy Burns.

'They're catheters, they've all got the Black Pox,' he said.

'What's that?'

'They've all caught gonorrhoea from black women. It's much worse than the pox you get from white women.'

'Will it get better?' I asked.

Paddy shook his head, 'No, there's no cure. They'll stay like that until they get to my age. Then their pricks will rot and they'll drop off.'

'Oh, Christ.' My eyes must have been popping out of my head with horror; at the time I believed this racist crap completely.

Paddy said. 'You're a good lad so you be careful. Don't you start that business.'

Start! Not bloody likely! My teeth were on edge and shudders were going up and down my spine. The aversion therapy was reinforced the first time I saw a man put the end of the catheter up his penis. I didn't wait to see how far it went or watch the purple Condy's Crystal Water coming out. No, I was vomiting in the heads. I didn't know whether you could catch this awful disease from a plate or cup, from having a pee in the same place or from sitting on a lavatory seat. I swear my penis shrunk two inches, I was afraid to expose it even for a pee. In the end Joe saw my distress and put me wise.

Before penicillin there was no completely effective cure for gonorrhoea. The sufferers would go to the steward for M&B tablets. I was amazed they could laugh; one man had a testicle swell up to the size of a cricket ball. The others made a joke of it, 'Hey, Danny's got a blue ball.' I wouldn't go near him, I was afraid that it might burst. Even worse, a joke went around about a girl approaching a seaman who had what was described as a 'full house,' gonorrhoea, syphilis and crabs.

'Hey there honey, do you want something new?' she asks.

'Hell, what have you got, leprosy?'

I was disgusted in a way only the young can be. I thought some of these men would be too old to want sex. I hated the atmosphere in the focs'le now. In my years at sea I never went with a prostitute, whether they were known as bar girls or by any other euphemism. I didn't become a saint, but I kept my hard-ons under control until we hit a home port. No virtue was involved it was unadulterated fear. I just wasn't an away player.

When we left port, it was positively a pleasure to go down to the stokehole and start shovelling again. Our next stop would be Durban in South Africa, which I was sure would be better. Come to think of it – that's the story of my life. The next port will always be wonderful.

Durban looked wonderful from the ship. We docked at The Bluff but only for twenty-four hours to fill the coal bunkers and we weren't allowed ashore. I stood at the rail and watched an odd sight. Black convicts, about two dozen of them, sparsely clad, were loading our coal under the supervision of two white guards with rifles. They wore white kepis, great big helmets. There were also two very large black guards, dressed in leopard skins, bare footed and carrying spears. I had a feeling of wonder as if I was looking at a scene of things long past.

I just couldn't stay on the ship. 'I'm going to try to get ashore,' I told Joe.

'I'll come with you.'

We went straight out through the gates with no challenge. We decided to walk towards Durban, which we guessed was about ten miles around the bay. On the way we passed through an Asian quarter that looked as I'd imagined India to be, not Africa. There were temples; colourful houses and the women wore saris.

We got into town at mid-morning and wandered happily about. Durban was a lovely, clean, modern city. Everything looked so new after the old buildings in England. I loved it. It seemed such a shame to have to go back to the horrible focs'le with the catheters.

'Joe, what do you think about going up to Johannesburg? They've got gold mines up there. We could get a job digging gold.'

'That's a good idea.' Joe was ready for anything.

This was our plan but unfortunately it didn't come to pass. A couple of plainclothes men approached us as we were strolling about.

'Linskey and Christie, I presume?' said one. They spoke weird English, which sounded a little like cockney.

'How did you know?' Joe asked.

'We've been on the lookout for you all day. You're being detained under the Prohibited Immigrants Act.'

'We only want to go and work in the goldmines,' said Joe.

'All the jobs there have been filled but your Captain desperately wants you back to help him run the ship.'

Their sarcasm seemed quite kindly though. The sergeant told us our ship had sailed and we would be sent down by train to meet the Albion in East London. We thought that would be all right; we'd be able to scarper up to Jo-burg. Then they said a policeman would accompany us.

We ate and slept in the police station that night. The copper who came with us next day was only a bit older than Joe. He was an avid cricket fan. Even when we said we didn't play, never had played and probably never would play, he kept on talking about it. Still, he seemed very generous, quite unlike any policeman I'd ever heard about.

'Would you like some lunch?' he asked, 'There's a diner on the train.'

'Yes, please,' we said eagerly. We had tea, soft drinks and chocolate. It was like being on a beano with a rich uncle like in the Boys' Adventure stories.

The countryside was wonderful. Some was cultivated but there were also miles of veldt. We saw zebra, deer and many different kinds of birds. We would see an occasional cluster of the round mud houses with pointed roofs. It was only about 250 miles I think--all too short--but I really enjoyed going through this strange land. What an exciting life this seagoing was, I thought. I was on top of the world with absolutely no worry about having to face the Commander. I thought he was stopping the ship in East London for us but it was to pick up part of our cargo of fruit of course.

We said good bye to our friendly copper at the ship, where the first mate said brusquely, 'Go and get cleaned up. Then come back here. I'll take you to the skipper.'

Commander Noakes was sitting behind a desk looking very stern. He just stared at us for a few minutes before speaking. 'Well, here you are again. I didn't want you on the ship in the first place. You took yourselves off the ship, now I've got you back on board. You're more bloody trouble than you're worth. Now, I'm going to log [fine] you first for disobeying the order to not go ashore.

'Next. I'm logging a day's pay for every day you missed, so I can pay the men who did your work. On top of that you have to pay all the expenses you've incurred. I have a bill from the South African Police.'

He read: 'Two single fares from Durban to East London. One return fare ditto for your guard, plus his wages, food and one-night stay in East London Hotel. Plus your food and drinks on the journey.

'You seem to have had quite a picnic. By the time you get off this ship you'll probably owe the company money. Go.'

We went. I said to Joe, 'No wonder that copper was so bloody generous.'

Joe said dreamily, 'It was worth it, wasn't it?'

Back to the focs'le and the jibes of the seamen. Later, one of them asked me, 'Did Joe have any fits while you were away?'

'What do you mean?'

'Joe has epileptic fits, didn't you know?'

No, I didn't. I'd never worked on the same watch as him and no one had mentioned it. I was glad he'd been all right, though; I wouldn't have known what to do. He did throw a wobbly a few days later, however, and someone had to put a wooden spoon in his mouth; it was quite frightening. Probably why he didn't get a second trip until he stowed away. This voyage finished his seagoing career and he died some months later. I heard that he talked all the time about his wonderful adventure in South Africa. Poor bugger.

Homeward bound! We saw Table Mountain from a distance. I thought that I would have gladly risked going ashore again had we been close enough. So would Joe. If we hadn't jumped off the ship in Durban, we wouldn't have ever set foot in South Africa or seen any of its delights. Impossible for any adventurer to resist. What's more, my father had fought in the Boer War and wouldn't have forgiven me if I hadn't had a look at the place. I've never forgotten that magic moment when I set foot ashore and, alas, I've never been able to recapture the same romantic feeling about anywhere else.

We had a brief bunkering stop in Dakar, French West Africa, which is now Senegal. It was hot, but after the Red Sea it was tolerable. It was another poor country and I could see nothing that looked inviting. Then many days later, we sailed into European waters and eventually arrived in Boulogne to discharge the cargo. We were allowed to go ashore and even got a couple of quid. France, although so close to home, I found really exciting. This was what I wanted abroad to be like. The smell of strong cigarettes, brandy, bread, and garlic hit my receptive nostrils. Nicely dressed women smelling of perfume clicked past on high heels. Accordions played and taxis hooted. Every French cliché came to life and it felt more foreign than Madagascar.

On our way home now, we didn't know whether the port would be Southampton, Liverpool or somewhere else. Then the buzz went that it was to be the Tyne and we were soon seeing familiar places.

The shipping master was coming aboard to pay the crew off. Joe and I had to go to the Captain first. He read out our list of fines, but then said, 'I'm going to scrub out all the things you've been logged for—misbehaving and absence without leave. You'll still have to pay all the expenses you and the policeman incurred on the journey from Durban to East London but I hope you appreciate how lenient I'm being. If I didn't scrub the fines, you'd have no money at all to show for your work.

'Furthermore, as it's your first trip and you're so young I'm not going to give you the bad discharge you deserve, otherwise you'd never get another berth. This way you can continue as seamen if you want to.'

We thanked him properly and said we did want to be seamen.

'Okay, Just do me a favour and DO NOT ever sign on to a ship under my command again. Go.'

So I landed as I'd often dreamed of doing. I was tanned, taller, fitter and I had £11 in my pocket. Not a vast fortune but more than I'd ever had at once in my life. Now I was a real man of the world. I'd even developed a sailor's roll.

PART 2
WAR IN THE ATLANTIC
1939-1944

Chapter 4
SS Kayla

My first stop was at the 'Fifty Shilling Tailors,' where I bought a bright green three-piece suit. The jacket was double-breasted with a back pleat each side to the waist and had a back belt. The style was called the Maxie Baer after the heavyweight champion boxer. I thought I was the bloody cat's whiskers, the envy of all the local youths and a magnet to the young girls. A veritable lady-killer.

Da greeted me with no surprise and I soon resumed my social round, except that now I'd meet the lads in the local and have a beer or two. I didn't like the taste much, but it seemed the thing to do. Da was delighted to drink with his rich son and after three weeks the money was gone, so I had to look for another ship.

I got a job on a coaster that ran coal down to Greenhythe on the Thames, where we picked up cement to bring back. I was told to provide my own pallet (straw mattress) and provisions. The company paid higher wages to compensate for this. Stupid as I was, I bought only a loaf of bread, a pound of butter and a pound of cheese, and didn't bother about a pallet, thinking I'd sleep rough.

I'd signed as a fireman and trimmer, which was usual on a small ship with only one boiler. By now I considered myself to be highly experienced after my one trip but it was really hard work. I had to do everything, because I'd replaced a man who'd gone off sick. He and the other two firemen had worked together on this regular run for years and they were extremely clannish. They hardly spoke to me; perhaps they thought I'd keep their mate's job. There was no chance of that. It was the hardest work I'd ever done in my life, and I alone was responsible for keeping steam up on my watch. Before this, someone else had always told me what to do.

The journey was only twenty-four hours, but it took nearly another eighteen to catch the tides. My food ran out before we left the docks and there was no more. I didn't blame the other firemen for not sharing their supplies; I'd only my own stupidity to blame and I learned a good lesson. I went without food for only about a day, but I worked two watches alone, hard work.

I was delirious with hunger by the time I managed to eat. Then a week later we were back in the Tyne and I had a few quid in my pocket again. I swore I'd never do another coastal run like that, but of course I did. Not immediately though. I was going home to climb into my bright green suit.

It wasn't there--Da had pawned it. He said it wasn't doing any good just taking up space in the house and I had to use some of my hard-earned cash to redeem it. When I was near the Pawn I saw one of the young girls I knew who was working there and was ashamed to go in. I went home with an earful of abuse for my father. 'Maggie Burke is working there, you silly sod. You'll have to get the suit out for me.'

He took the money and went. On his return he said, 'Maggie asked if Billie was home again.'

The shame of it, I thought. 'Don't you do that again. You leave my suit alone.'

'All right,' he said, 'Next time I'll go to Hoppers with it.'

I loved that suit, but every time I was out of the house for five minutes it was in the Pawn. However, one day I came back home and it was two sizes too small for me; I had grown dramatically. Like boots and other things it went on its final journey. My father complained bitterly about his loss of income.

Out in the world, great events were taking place. Although I was regarded as a tearaway, I was well read on current events and political trends and had formed political leanings to the left. This was more because of my dislike of fascism, which had spread all over Europe, than any great love of communism. I wasn't sure I liked any '-ism.'

Japan invaded China in 1931-32, Mussolini conquered Ethiopia in 1935 and the Spanish Civil War started in July 1936. The English wouldn't help the democratically elected Republican government and declared it illegal for any British subjects to join the Popular Front Army or for ships to break Fascist Franco's blockade. They wouldn't offer protection to any subject who flouted their orders.

An English ship owner known as Potato Jones had been condemned to death in absentia by Franco. His crime had been buying up old wrecks of ships and filling them with provisions for the Front. (One of these ships, the SS Gloxinia, to my certain knowledge, had been rusting in the Tyne since the Great War.) I was offered a berth on a similar wreck, the *SS Kayla*.

By this time, the Popular Front was getting a pasting, though they still held an area around Barcelona. We were taking a general cargo there. For this unofficial trip there was no shipping Master, so we signed on aboard. We were to get bonus danger money. Signing on wasn't any act of heroism on my part, nor even an expression of my political beliefs. I simply knew that I wasn't going to be hurt and I needed the money.

We sailed out at night, bound for Marseilles. The hold was full of potatoes for ballast as well as cargo. That's how Potato Jones got his nickname, he liked potatoes better than coal because they were cleaner. At Marseilles, however, the French wouldn't let us land; the new cargo was loaded very quickly and we sailed the next morning. Franco's Navy was supposed to be around but we didn't sight them. We unloaded whatever it was at night in Barcelona, where everyone seemed hurried and furtive. We heard the thump of big guns but it was only about as loud as washing day in Jarrow and no more exciting.

It had been planned to make a regular run to Barcelona, but the war finished and Franco started his long Fascist dictatorship. It was now March 1939 and I'd had my eighteenth birthday at sea. Nothing much seemed to be happening. Since the Munich pact, there had been a lull but no one believed Hitler would stop his aggression. They were sure there would be a war. Sandbags were filled and trenches dug. The authorities issued Anderson shelters to each house, which they claimed were easy for two people to erect. That was true enough except that you needed a bloody great hole three feet deep first. The shelters were about seven by five feet, a bit difficult for Grandmas to help with. They made plenty of work for navvies.

I couldn't get a ship for weeks so I decided to go to London, where I found work as a stoker in the Royal Free Hospital and lived with Sheila and her new husband, Paddy O'Hara.

When Hitler invaded Poland in August, I returned to Jarrow. I was very restless and I thought there would be plenty of ships moving about. But there wasn't much doing, even when War was declared in September. A U-boat sank the Glasgow Liner Athenia on the day the war broke out, and in retaliation the RAF bombers dropped six million leaflets on Germany calling for Hitler's surrender. Must have terrified them.

I took a job at a builder's where I dug holes, filled sandbags and installed Anderson Shelters, then filled more sandbags, dug more holes and installed more Anderson shelters. Things were still quiet in England. No one seemed much concerned that the German Army was rapidly jack-booting its way across Europe. The whisper was that the war would be over by Christmas. Some hope!

For the first time in years many men got jobs; war had cured the depression. Shipyards were reopening and there was unlimited work; even old men could join the ARP (Air Raid Precautions), where they could get a nice uniform and have a bit of authority. A few layabouts I knew even became Special Constables. In all, a sort of euphoria settled on the country and there was plenty of drinking money around.

Sketches about funny Hitler with his little moustache were rolling them in the aisles in the music halls. Songs like 'Run, Hitler, Run' (to the tune of 'Run Rabbit, Run') were going to have us 'Hang out our washing on the Seigfried Line.' No one seemed to notice Hitler was running towards us, not away. In October a battleship, The Royal Oak, was sunk by a torpedo in her home base at Scapa Flow. Hitler had overrun Europe and trapped the British Expeditionary Army on the beaches of Dunkirk.

I had at last got a couple of berths on the coastal trips I disliked so much and was in Cardiff when I read of the Dunkirk evacuation in 1940. It was certainly a wonderful effort by many brave sailing men to rescue the troops. Theirs was the only victory, although somehow the rout was depicted as a great triumph for England. This was the end of the phoney war and now the war on shipping started, the aim of which was to stop supplies and starve Britain out. Britain's survival depended on the merchant ships getting through.

Winston Churchill said in one of his most famous rallying speeches: 'The Battle of the Atlantic was the dominating factor all through the war. Never for one moment could we ever forget that everything else depended on its outcome.' However, he showed no signs of these sentiments in his treatment of the Merchant Service when the war was on. The Luftwaffe attacked a convoy in the English Channel and U-boats and E-boats joined in. E-boats were fast little motor launches, so that the onslaught came from every quarter. It was a massacre.

Chapter 5
SS Marconi

When I went to the labour exchange to sign on for the dole, I was sent to the Shipping Federation in Shields. They directed me to the SS Marconi. Owned by Lambert and Holt, she had been a Blue Funnel boat, her cargo mainly bananas from West Africa. She hadn't been to sea for a couple of years. Now that the war was being taken seriously, we seamen were on the payroll, either on board ship or in 'the Pool,' which was the working register for available seamen who could take the next ship in their home port. If they were needed elsewhere for crew they could be sent anywhere in the UK. The pay was £10, two shillings and sixpence a month. We got one day off for every month served and then went straight back into the Pool for another berth. If we were unlucky enough to sign off far away from our home port, we wouldn't have time to return home for months sometimes. Some of the peacetime seamen wanted to join the army so as at least to be on dry land for the duration but were unable to get a release from the Merchant Marine. We were held to be essential to the war effort and once in you stayed in.

The Marconi was a large ship with a big crew, among which I was delighted to find a lot of my Jarrow mates. Harry McIver, Tommy Devine, and Paddy Connelly I knew well, and Tommy Smalley was an old acquaintance. It was just as well--we were going to need a bit of light entertainment. Paddy Connelly had been sent to an industrial school, probably for truancy, and he'd learned to stand up for himself there. He was handsome and looked slightly Mediterranean as do so many Irish, although bright blue eyes gave him away. He and Tommy Devine both had a wicked sense of humour. And they were tough; no one messed with them in Jarrow. Nor with me come to think of it. It was just as well that we were mates; we could have killed each other in a fight.

In October 1940, we went North to Loch Ewe in Scotland to pick up our convey. We didn't know where we were bound because all ships were under sealed orders that wouldn't be opened until we were at sea. I was excited when I heard we were going to Buenos Aires.

At the beginning the convoys were small and were only escorted about 200 miles out. After that the ships went off at their own speed, zigzagging to avoid torpedoes. We headed towards North America, then turned South, staying near the coast all the way and sometimes seeing a bit of land or a mountain in the distance. From England it took six weeks and we didn't stop anywhere. It was dead boring.

We went on water and food rations about ten days before we arrived. The ship went on and on and on. Harry McIver and Tommy Smalley had ulcers and constantly discussed their symptoms. Harry had a miserable face and Tommy was a nervous, tense little man. The ulcers didn't prevent them from drinking heavily and the next day they were practically bed-ridden with agony. Nor did this stop them from going back for more punishment. Devine and Connelly teased them mercilessly. When we reached Buenos Aires, they disappeared into the Boca, the bar area on the opposite side of the River Plate. The rest of us covered for them in cleaning the fires and the boxes, although I for one was dying to get ashore.

When we entered the River Plate, we saw the turret of the German battleship *Graf Spey* sticking up out of the water. Cornered by the British on December 17th 1939, the captain had scuttled the giant ship and then committed suicide. There wasn't much admiration of his bravery on our ship. 'One less bastard to blow us up,' an old sailor commented when someone remarked on the captain's courage.

There in Buenos Aires the cruise of my lifetime started. It was a beautiful and glamorous city, where the music of the Tango beat in the air. They danced in every bar and wherever there was a piece of smooth uncobbled pavement. The men were gallant and the señoritas flirtatious. Steaks covered the dinner plates--gorgeous mouth-watering beef—and all the food was wonderful. The first words of Spanish I learned were relevant to food of course: *pany manteca* (bread and butter), *tocino* (bacon), huevos y papas fritas (eggs and chips). I could have eaten the eggs and bacon until I started cackling. I was drinking a glass of wine with meals and the occasional beer but I didn't take to spirits much. They seemed to make me drunk very quickly and I didn't like losing control.

First we loaded cargo in Encinada, then at Berisso and La Plata on the way back out to sea. They were all small heavens, as far as I was concerned, with wonderful people in them, although I had one less welcoming experience. Rather than spend all the time in bars, I used to go for long exploratory walks. During one such walk, I went into an ordinary looking bar for a cold beer. It was weird. No one spoke to me and even the barman didn't look in my direction. He didn't insult me nor explicitly refuse to serve me but I simply didn't exist for him. The customers were respectable looking men, mostly middle-aged and wearing business suits. No one met my eye and I felt like H.G. Wells's Invisible Man. As I was sober I didn't even bother to complain but just walked out. I looked back from the door to find every expressionless face staring at me. Then I saw the explanation in a room at the side, which had a whole wall of Nazi flags and memorabilia around a massive painting of Hitler. I knew there were thousands of Germans in Argentina. I had just met some of them.

Another time in La Plata, I'd split from my mates and gone for a walk to get drunk with an Argentinean. I woke up in jail with hazy memories of different bars. The jail consisted of a concrete blockhouse with just two cells and an office set in the middle of a field. The sun was lashing down and my head was pounding. My mouth was as dry as the Sahara and tasted like a cesspit. I was nearly delirious for want of a drink of cold clear water. I banged on the bars and a warder came. He belonged to the *marineros* (dock police) and was dressed in a naval type uniform. An extremely sullen man, he didn't speak.

"Agua, please,' I croaked, 'Please some water."

He just gave me an evil grin, spat on the floor and walked away with what I think was the equivalent of 'Bollocks' on his tongue. I hated the sadistic bastard.

The First Mate arrived at about 11:00 am to pay my fine and get me out. The fine was later deducted from my wages. I had a bad lump on the side of my eye, God knows where from.

'This is the first time I've been in jail through drink,' I told him.

"Better make bloody sure it's the last too."

Despite his lack of sympathy, he took me to a bar where he had a beer and I drank about a gallon of cold water. I was often to wish I'd taken his advice but despite my thirst I felt like 'one of the boys' at last. They were always having adventures.

In Buenos Aires immigration officials had brought a Pole to the ship. He'd been picked up as an illegal immigrant and the court had ordered his deportation. As the Germans now occupied his country, we couldn't understand what he was doing on an English ship until we found out that he didn't want to go home but to join the Free Polish troops in England. The captain agreed that he could take the place of a trimmer who was in hospital in BA

Vlad spoke Spanish as well as Polish, but no one in the focs'le spoke either of these languages and our firemen's brand of Geordie didn't sound much like English, either. Vlad and I could communicate a bit, though, because I was picking up some Spanish.

We were in Argentina for nearly four weeks before sailing to Monte Video in Uruguay. Devine, Harry and Tommy Smalley had the taste for booze by now and they went adrift, finishing up in jail. Devine was a powerful man who liked to laugh. He loved to fight even more and was a better man to have on your side than the opposing one. He walked with a swagger and really got up the noses of many who fancied themselves as tough. He was a ferocious fighter and constantly exercised to keep fit. The three of them had had a good brawl with the locals but the police won it finally and incarcerated them, which left the boiler cleaning for Vlad and me.

The *Marconi* hadn't sailed far so it wasn't too long a job. When it was done, Vlad suggested we have a drink ashore, where we got quite matey. In the same pub were some German sailors who had been crew on *The Graf Spey*. But there was no animosity between us seamen and no fighting broke out. They were waiting for passage home to Germany, but please God they said, not too soon.

Our cruise of South America took us up the coast to Rio Grande do Sol in Brazil next. We bunkered there and so had only about twenty-four hours. I went ashore with Vlad again and we had a couple of beers; then he excused himself to make a phone call. He came back to tell me that he had some relatives a little way out that he was going to visit and would I like to come with him? I certainly would. He'd called a taxi and it took us on a thirty-minute ride through some prosperous suburbs.

He got a rapturous greeting from about ten people, who made me welcome too. The booze came out--spirits mainly--and masses of food. One old lady--his granny I think--kept hugging him and talking very seriously. Whatever she said got the nodding approval of everyone.

I really shouldn't have drunk spirits, because after some time I was conscious of being in a taxi and then of nothing else until I woke in my bunk next morning. Vlad's family must have brought me back. The ship was moving but his bunk was empty.

'Where's the Pole?' the Chief Engineer asked me.

I explained what had happened but he just nodded. 'Oh well, he's gone for the duration if he's got any sense.'

We had to sail short-handed. I was sick with frustration. If I'd known that Vlad had planned to stay in Brazil, nothing in this world would have dragged me back to the Marconi. Lack of communication had scuppered me. Perhaps he or his family had thought I might shop him and so didn't confide in me. In Rio de Janeiro we were allowed ashore for a brief few hours, just long enough to see Sugar Loaf Mountain and Copocabana Beach. The last stop was Recife in Permanbuco, which was approached through long straits filled by hundreds of wooden windjammers with tall masts and sails. I'd fallen in love with South America and never wanted to leave. It had warmth, good food, beautiful women and friendly people. What more could any man want?

Now we were homeward bound, sailing east to the convoy port of Freetown, Sierra Leone. Although we were alone in the Atlantic we weren't afraid of German subs or raiders. The Ocean was so vast we thought it would be terribly bad luck if one found us.

The day after we sailed I found Harry McIver sitting on the side of his bunk; his face was even longer than usual. 'Bill, am I morose?' he asked.

I wasn't sure what the word meant, so I stalled. 'Why do you ask?'

'Devine said I always looked morose. I can tell you he'd look bloody morose if he had my stomach. My ulcer's bloody killing me.'

'Jesus, Harry, what do you expect? You haven't drawn a sober breath for six weeks. Your poor damn ulcer must be screaming for mercy.'

At least I now knew what the word meant. 'Yes, Harry, you do look morose.'

We arrived safely in Freetown, where we lay out to bunker. We joined the convoy and waited a few days to collect about forty more ships; then we were homeward bound and well protected. About four days after we left, at around six one morning, there was a blood-curdling scream from the tween decks. A trimmer called Jimmy Walsh was there, shovelling coal into the pocket, which took it to the bunker below. Suddenly he saw the coal moving of its own accord and then in the middle of it a pair of eyes and white teeth. The light was dim down there and Jimmy screamed in terror. Then the teeth began speaking and an entire black body materialised out of the coal.

The stowaway was one of the stevedores who had been loading our coal. He must have run out of water and food days earlier because he was famished. He was also scared to death and had no idea what might happen to him. God knows why he wanted to go to Europe in wartime but perhaps anything was better than the poverty of Freetown. He was a good-looking lad of about seventeen.

As we couldn't see the dirt on him, the trimmer took him straight to breakfast and introduced him to Devine and the other firemen.

We called him Joe. When he'd stuffed more food into himself than I'd ever seen anyone put away, he looked much happier. Jimmy Walsh went to report the incident and the mate said to bring him to the Captain at ten o'clock. The Captain gave him a job in the galley, where they were glad to get him. He was a good worker and always happy. He became a British seaman.

On Christmas Day we were given a special meal and a small bottle of spirits each. Devine had inside knowledge and cornered the market on these small bottles before anyone else knew that there would be an issue. We'd seen him buying sweets in the slops and thought he'd gone nuts but later he bought all the bottles from the ten youngsters - new cabin and galley boys who didn't drink - for a handful of these sweets. The lucky bugger was drunk for a couple of days.

I'd almost deluded myself that the war had gone away, but it was back with us quickly enough. We left behind Liverpool and Birkenhead and sailed up the Mersey through the Manchester Ship Canal. We were able to call out to people on the towpath. I'll never forget the awe on Joe's face; even with the bombing it looked very impressive.

The ninety miles to Salford took about twenty-four hours going slowly with a pilot; then we had to stay on board for customs and immigration. After that, the Dockers swarmed on and started unloading. The place was a hive of activity; the hatches were off and the big cranes were delving in to discharge the cargo.

By 6:00 p.m. we lined up for an advance on our wages and went ashore. Devine had bought a monkey from one of the coal stevedores in Freetown. It was a lovely little thing and became a source of much entertainment in the focs'le. He called it Jacko and cuddled it like a baby. Devine took it off the ship concealed under his jacket and we surrounded him going out the gate, not that anyone was very interested in quarantine in war time. The nearest pub was the Clewes so we piled in there. The landlord was enchanted with Jacko and asked Devine to sell him. 'Never,' he answered. 'I love this little fellow better than anything in the world. I'd rather sell my wife.'

'Thanks, but I've already got one of those,' said the publican. 'If you change your mind, come back.'

We went to a couple more pubs and looked round at the bomb damage. Manchester, Liverpool and the whole Mersey area had been blitzed by 400 bombers a couple of weeks earlier. There were an awful lot of blank spaces where houses used to stand.

The monkey was getting to be a bit of a worry because the responsibility of being a nanny was curtailing Devine's drinking. 'I'd like to put Jacko somewhere quiet for a bit,' he said.

'What about the left luggage at the railway station?' someone suggested.
That seemed like a good idea so we all trooped down there. When Devine brought the monkey out from his coat, the uniformed porter looked astonished.

'Ee lad, can't leave moonkey 'ere, would tear up parcels.'

Devine promised that Jacko would behave. A superior rank came over. 'What's oop? What's that?' 'It's moonkey. He wants to book in moonkey.'

'Ee, he can't leave moonkey 'ere.'

So Devine had to keep Jack with him. The monkey liked being with people and had become spoilt rotten on the trip over. The porters' Manchester accent sounded hilarious to us Geordies; for years whenever we bumped into each other we'd greet each other with: 'You can't leave moonkey 'ere."

Needless to say, we thought our own accent was spot-on English.

The sirens went off announcing an air raid. People rushed to find shelters and pretty soon the streets were deserted. We heard a rattling piano in one pub and went in. Everyone was drinking and singing and it looked quite a good party so we stayed.

Then the most unholy sound reached our ears. Hundreds of German bombers were attacking the city, aiming especially at the docks. As it was our first experience of an air raid, we fought our way out through the heavy blackout curtains to have a look. Bombs were falling all around from wave after wave of bombers - the papers next day said 400. Then they went on to the next target down the Canal. I was a bit scared but not as terrified as I might have been. I'm not sure whether it was Dutch courage or just the fact that I had land and not fathoms of cold water under my feet. The water mains had been damaged and the fires raged out of control for a while. We didn't actually see any bomb hit but I noticed plenty of rescue workers clearing up the aftermath.

Eventually we went back to the Marconi. We were paid off the next day and Devine reluctantly decided that he would have to part with Jacko, who was proving too much responsibility for a drinking man. So he took him to the Clews pub, where money changed hands.

We had to take four trains to get to Jarrow. The lines had been blown up in different places and there were many detours. It was standing room only most of the way. The carriages were full of soldiers with enormous kit bags going from one place to another. God knows why; the Army wasn't doing any fighting at that time. I

took my father for a drink and we ran into Devine and Smalley.
Devine was crying drunk about the loss of his little monkey friend.
'I've betrayed him,' he cried.

Smalley tried to comfort him. 'You've done the right thing
Tommy; it was no sort of life for the wee creature. He's gone to a
very good safe home.'

Devine, the violent fighting man, had been humbled by a
monkey.

Chapter 6
SS Zelo and *SS.Newbury*

Da told me that Sheila had been bombed out, so after my leave I asked for a coastal trip to London. I sailed on the *S.S.Zelo*. We went in a convoy, which was very slow but fairly well protected. A submarine managed to sink a ship but not one near us. By now all convoys were really slow, not only because of their speed at sea but through waiting so long in port. All the ships would have to come to a meeting point, for example the Tyne. There would be at least two convoys going down the coast each week and your ship might wait there two days for one. A destroyer and perhaps a sloop would protect the convoy. On the way, perhaps at Hull or Grimsby, more ships would come out to join the convoy. All the coasters were slow but we had to sail at the speed of the slowest. To reduce their speed further they had to zigzag. We could count on about a week in all, with loading and waiting, to get down the coast from Tyneside to London, when the sailing was really only about thirty-six hours.

Coasters were sunk almost every day of the week even though the skippers knew every wave in the sea and had been sailing it since they were boys. The east and south coasts were a graveyard of ships. Wreckage that showed was the best; you worried about what you couldn't see under the water. Close to the coast the haphazard dropping of mines was a terrible menace. The newest designs were magnetic mines, which were drawn to the ships' metal hulls. Minesweepers would clear the lanes in front of the convoys and lookouts were posted, but the mines were free floating and it wasn't possible get rid of all of them. Many ships were lost in this way.

The *Zelo* stokehole crew were Spanish refugees from the Civil War. I was okay with them because I'd run the blockade with Potato Jones. We docked at Rochester and I decided I'd stay in London for a while. I packed my kit and left it near my bunk but the ship pulled out to the buoys. I managed to get on the shore boat but I couldn't take my bag with me. I went by train to London and traced Sheila through the nearest pub. She and Paddy had lodgings in a big house in King's Cross and there was a spare room for me.

That night there was one of the worst air raids so far on London. They concentrated on the East End and the Docks. Silvertown, across the Thames from Greenwich, was practically flattened. Despite all the houses that were knocked down every night during the Blitz, there was always plenty of accommodation; everyone that could had evacuated their families to the safety of the countryside.

I wrote to my father asking him to pick up my kit bag when the *Zelo* returned to the Tyne. His return letter said he was glad I wasn't dead; the Spanish had heard of the London raid and knew that was where I'd gone. When I didn't return to the ship they were sure I'd been killed.

Hitler occupied all of Europe now and had even taken the Channel Islands, which was considered a bit too close for comfort. The real Blitz started in September and while London was the worst and most consistently raided, all the major cities took a belting at some time. The RAF did a terrific job, although it seemed at one time that every plane must have been shot out of the sky. Churchill made an announcement that Britain was 'bristling' with two million soldiers with rifles and bayonets in their hands ready to resist invasion.

Sheila's husband Paddy worked in the rescue service and became a hefty drinker. It was a very distressing job and he never became hardened to people crying for their dead and trying to pull masonry away with their bare hands. Digging out the dead and badly injured living bodies was horror. Sometimes the most upset people, probably suffering from shock, were crying for their lost possessions. Sheila, on the other hand, never gave a damn about her bits and pieces. In all, she was bombed out four times and by the time the Blitz ended she could have fitted everything she owned into carrier bag.

I took a job as a stoker in a hospital but was afraid I wouldn't be able to do it for long before the authorities caught up with me and sent me back to sea. When I got home after one night shift, bugger me, Sheila had been bombed out again. I thought Fate was giving me a nudge, so I went to the Shipping Office in Lemann Street, Aldgate and signed on the Pool. The next day I was on another coaster going back to the Tyne. They were so desperate for crew that the shipping company agent took me by taxi to the ship in Tilbury Docks, down river. We passed through rows of flattened old houses. These bombed out places had been dreadful bug-ridden slums and Hitler had achieved in this case a quite welcome type of final solution. Everyone cried for the dead but not for the houses.

We arrived safely in the Tyne after the usual dive bomber attack on the convoy. This time they just dropped their bombs, missed and buggered off.

SS Newbury

In March 1941, I joined the *SS Newbury* for another Atlantic run. The danger from mines and aircraft had lessened but the submarine threat increased. Deep-sea convoys were even slower than coastal ones to get away. From the Tyne, the ship would zigzag its own way up the coast to the Firth of Forth in Scotland, where it would join whatever ships were already there. Then it would wait for other ships coming from other places like London and Hull. When between ten and fifteen had gathered, they would then go in convoy to Loch Ewe on the west coast of Scotland, protected by four or five destroyers and probably a couple of mine-sweepers. They would join the others lying there and have to wait perhaps a couple of weeks for yet more ships. This large convoy might have a battleship and if it was lucky a dozen Destroyers, minesweepers and a couple of sloops. Then it would head for North America, zigzagging all the way.

The *SS Newbury* ran unescorted up to Methil in the Firth of Forth without attack. We were only there for two days but in that time we saw thousands of Poles. They'd managed to get away from Poland to join the Polish Free Army, later to become known as Sikorsky's Army, which suffered heavy casualties in the war. At this time they didn't speak a word of English. Churchill's 'two million soldiers' consisted of men from every occupied country as well as all the Empire troops. They all had to be fed somehow.

Our convoy numbered about sixteen and was escorted to Loch Ewe on the West Coast. Other ships kept arriving and after two weeks we had the full complement, about twenty-five in all. I can remember only one cruiser in our escort but a hell of a lot of destroyers which were really fast and scurried round and among the convoy like border collies herding stray sheep; this was very comforting.

I'd sailed with a couple of the crew before but none were close friends. The donkeyman, Jock McBain, who seemed particularly old, had been torpedoed twice during World War I and had stayed in the service in the intervening years. We had a Bofors gun this time and two soldiers to man it but Jock McBain regretted its presence.

'Why don't you like it?' we asked. 'Surely it gives us a chance to fire back?'

'Because last war,' he said, 'the subs would come alongside and tell us to abandon ship and get into the lifeboats. They'd tell us they were going to radio our position so we could be picked up. Then they blew up the ship and we were rescued. We were civilians then, but with that Bofors gun we've become combatants.'

'After they put those useless bloody guns on our ships, a few clever dick officers waited until the sub came up alongside and blew it out of the water. After that we were just bombarded and we didn't have a chance.'

Someone said, 'Well, after all that's what we're supposed to do. It's wartime - we're supposed to kill the enemy.'

McBain snorted. 'You've got it all wrong, son. You're not in the bloody Royal Navy. You're a bloody sea-going navvy and your only job is to get the bloody ship from one bloody port to another.'

We were heading towards Canada again, feeling fairly safe because convoys were usually attacked on the way home when they were low and slow in the water with a full load. But these subs couldn't resist having a go at us; they must have been waiting in the shipping lane in the hope of seeing a returning convoy. Better to sink an empty ship than no ship, I suppose.

The siren went off, warning of an approaching submarine and calling us to action stations. Then I heard depth charges for the first time. The convoy was sailing in columns of five and over the far side from us a ship was blown up.

Then another.

I was on my watch down in the stokehole when it started. The depth charges started far away and came closer. The sound was like someone banging on a big empty tank with a sledgehammer, the vibration sending shudders throughout the ship. The noise was terrific.

I was apprehensive, but I can't say now that I was really shit scared. At one point I looked at the bulkhead and thought how thin it was. I imagined a torpedo coming through and blowing me to smithereens. Then I said to myself, 'No, No, I'm safe. I'm a spectator, a civilian. I don't want to fight.'

One of the depth charges made a direct hit on a sub in front of the convoy. By the time our ship passed near the spot, we could see oil and debris on the surface but no submariners. If there were more, they scarpered and the convoy sailed on. The subs set up another small raid within twenty-four hours but I guess there simply weren't enough of them. The wolf packs would come much later.

As on my earlier trip we turned south after reaching the North American coast. I was elated to hear that we were going to Buenos Aires again. We had crossed the Equator when all the crew mustered on deck for a talk by the Captain. The off-watch firemen crawled unwillingly out of their bunks, muttering some nasty words about officers and their bloody thoughtlessness. They didn't even bother getting dressed.

The Captain was a retired Royal Navy Officer, about sixty years old and terribly gung-ho. He faced the crew with his uniform spotless, gold buttons gleaming and his chin bravely held high though his hopes must have been low as he viewed his rabble firemen.

'Men, I have an announcement to make. I have been informed that the German battleship, the *Bismark*, is in this vicinity. If we sight it, we shall engage it. I expect you to do your duty, as British seamen.'

'This prick thinks he's bloody Nelson,' someone muttered.

There was a dead silence. The Bismark was one of the heaviest battleships ever armoured. It had Christ knows how many sixteen-inch cannons and every other kind of weapon imaginable. They said it could sink a ship twenty miles away. We had the equivalent of a bow and arrow.

The old donkeyman, Jock McBain was standing next to me.

'Hey Bill, what did he say?'

'He said we're going to attack the *Bismark*. He thinks that maybe we can sink it.'

Jock went crazy, 'You stupid old fucker, you'll get us all killed!' he shouted. 'We're bloody civilians!'

The Captain's face was purple. 'If this was the Navy, I'd have you put in irons! I'll deal with you later. Crew dismissed.'

The off-duty crew went back to their bunks and the rest of us discussed our forthcoming ordeal. 'The crazy bastard wants to get a medal,' said one. 'It'll be bloody posthumous,' said another. 'All we'll get'll be a watery grave.'

For at least a week the atmosphere was tense. We watched for any suspicious change in our zigzagging pattern but nothing happened. We decided the danger had passed and someone else would have to sink the Bismark. Of course, the Navy did that later.

Jock was heavily fined for disrespectful conduct.

When we reached Buenos Aires, the wreck of the *Graf Spey* was still there on the River Plate. It would stay for a long time and become a landmark as well known to seamen as the Statue of Liberty. We went into dry dock for repairs that would take eight days. This dock was only walking distance from the Plaza de Mayo, the square which would later be the site of the dreadfully sad marches by the mothers and families of the victims of *Los Desparecedos,* the disappeared victims of the Military Junta in the seventies. Right now, however, it was a place of fun and tango music. Jock seemed to have a lot of money to spend and was excessively and uncharacteristically generous, buying us wonderful meals and drinks.

We went upriver to Rosario and Villa Constitution, where we loaded general cargo. Then we continued up a tributary of the River Plata to the town of Parana and from there to La Paz, before heading for home via the Virgin Islands.

I was sitting with Jock one evening waiting for our watch to start. 'I really appreciate all the meals and booze you bought me in the Argentine, Jock,' I said. 'Where in Christ's name did you get all the money?'

'Well, keep it to yourself. I struck a gold mine.'

He'd only been made donkeyman on this trip; before that he'd been a fireman. The promotion gave him a cabin on his own. The previous donkeyman had been a loner who'd hardly been off the ship for years; when it was laid up, he'd stayed on board as watchman. For some unknown reason, however, on the last trip he'd gone ashore in Buenos Aires, where he was knocked down and killed by a truck. It was rumoured that he had been robbed, as there was no money on him.

Jock had inherited his job and his small private cabin. There was a piece of wooden panelling between the bunk and the bulkhead and as he was lying in bed one night he saw a space. He put his hand down and found an envelope, full of money. He didn't tell me how much but said it was a lot, all of the donkeyman's savings.

Jock established that the donkeyman had no family and had left no will. He then decided that if he handed the money in, only the officer's mess would benefit or the company would keep it. 'So, Bill, I said to myself, 'Sod that' and spent it all on my mates. If anything happens, at least we've had a last good piss-up.'

When we reached St. Thomas in the Virgin Islands, we were not allowed off the ship. Jock still had some money left and a thirst upon him. 'Come ashore with me,' he urged, so along with Billy Duncan, another fireman, we did. The rum was nectar. We started on tart drinks with fruit juice and mint but soon got down to the nitty gritty and drank neat rum. It seemed to suit the hot climate. As we strolled to the next bar we met a couple of AWOL Scandinavian seamen who took us to buy bottles of hooch and showed us their favourite drinking place under an empty house. The houses were built on stilts, which made a wonderful shady shelter and the Danes were wild drinkers. The party grew. When it thinned out eventually, I went off with a half-full bottle under my arm and fell asleep in the shade of a tree. By the time I woke, the shade had moved and I was in the full glare of the sun. I was in agony, burning, burning everywhere. I thought it was sunburn, until I realised I was covered in big ants, which were chewing lumps out of me. I tore all my clothes off and shook the ants off them; then I put my trousers back on and hurried to the ship. My back and arms were the worst; I had hundreds of bites. I'd been lying right on top of the ant hole. I was on fire.

I got scant sympathy back on board, but the Steward cleaned and dressed my wounds and gave me some ointment to use. I had to stand my watch because the ship was leaving. That was agonising-- the stings in the heat and the sweat. Oh, my God, the pain! It didn't abate for a week.

Jock and Billy Duncan had also been rounded up and returned to the ship. The next morning we were hauled in front of our Gung Ho captain. 'I'm charging you under the Defence of the Realm Act with being Absent without Leave and disobeying orders. You'll appear in a civilian court when we return to the U.K.'

Again we crossed the Atlantic alone and joined another big convoy at Freetown. This time we were attacked several different times as we got closer to home and lost two ships from the convoy. The enemy would fire a torpedo, upon which the destroyers would get after them. Then it would be quiet for a few hours until we heard the siren again.

The battle of the Atlantic was really heating up now. The *Bismark* had been hounded to death by the Royal Navy and sunk! It was a fitting revenge for the sinking of the 42,000-ton, *H.M.S. Hood,* the pride of the British Fleet. It was also one big sod less for us to worry about.

We docked in London this time. I was pleased, because I wanted to see Sheila. The usual Customs and Immigration came aboard; it took a particularly long time and we waited about for hours. Jock, Billy and I thought we may have been let off the hook, but the police came aboard and arrested us. They took us to West Ham Police Station and charged us with some obscure wartime law. We got six weeks in jail, of which I served four. Jock and Billy went to Wormwood Scrubs but I was under twenty-one so I was sent to a

Young Persons' Prison at Feltham, which had been a Borstal before the war. Now it was run under Army type discipline.

Our barracks were for young servicemen who'd been AWOL or had committed a minor military crime, which was an easy thing to do in the army with all their stupid bloody rules. We slept in six-bunk dormitories, one of which I shared with some Canadian soldiers. We were kept well apart from the civilian prisoners. I suppose they thought we were undisciplined enough without learning any more bad habits.

It turned out to be the most wonderful time I'd had in my life. The whole of the British Islands was under cultivation; every square foot of soil behind little houses held a couple of plants. They sent us convicts out to work on the land. It was July and the most fabulous weather. We'd strip down as far as possible whilst getting in the crop. After the day's work, we returned to delicious meals, young men's meals of stews, soups and roasts, while there was rationing for the poor bloody civilians outside.

I wanted to stay there forever, but alas all good things come to an end. The trouble was I behaved too bloody well and only had to serve four weeks of the six. When they turned me out, I went to the shipping office to sign off and get my pay from the *S.S. Newbury*.

'The *Newbury*?' repeated The Office Manager. 'You're a lucky bastard aren't you?'

I was puzzled; this wasn't the usual penpusher's reaction to jail sentences. 'Why?' I asked.

'The *Newbury* sailed towards Cardiff and was sunk. All hands were lost.'

'Oh Christ.' It was like a kick in the gut. Crews become good friends working in such close quarters.

I told him about the Captain and the *Bismark*.

'It sounds as though the Captain was a brave man, perhaps too brave' said the clerk.

'God rest their souls.' I said.

I met up with Jock and Billy Duncan, whose sentences had also been shortened and that night we got stocious. We were sorry about the lads and drank to them but we celebrated our own survival as well.

Chapter 7
SS Ashby

I went to Jarrow by train and took the four days leave owing to me. At the time clothes rationing was on and clothes coupons were as good as money. I don't know why but we seamen were given a lot of them, which we sold. I had a good leave on the proceeds.

Then I signed on for a coastal trip to Portsmouth. As I say, I hated the coastal trips because you had to buy your own food. Never a domesticated man, I was absolutely unable to look after myself and certainly didn't want to spend any of my shore leave going with a little bag to a grocery store. Sometimes, however, I'd manage to buy some bread, eggs and bacon to put in my locker in the focs'le. Then I'd have to take it to the galley where there were pots and pans, and cook it on the hot-plate. I'd have to clean up after myself too. Deep seamen were used to working hard, having a wash, eating lots of hot, well-cooked grub and then turning in to sleep. This arduous distraction drove me mad. I don't think that on any occasion I bought enough food and I finished up every trip feeling starved to death. I used to promise myself that if I were unfortunate to be sent again on one of these trips I'd buy a proper amount. In the next breath, I'd promise myself I'd never do a home trip again.

The convoy went safely until we reached 'E-Boat Alley,' as it was called, an area of the English Channel between Dover and Southampton. The fast little E-Boats would come out from French ports, fire at the convoys and then rush back. They did a terrible lot of damage. They fired on our convoy and while the destroyers were chasing them away a dive-bomber attacked us.

I was down below when we heard the banshee scream of the plane and the din of our ship and the escort ship firing back. The bombs missed. Actually I think they mostly did miss, but the sound of the planes diving was terrifying. In my stupidity I'd rather shrugged off the danger of air attacks, reserving all my fears for U-boats or mines, of which there were plenty around the coast.

In June 1941 the Germans invaded Russia. The general feeling was that Hitler had gone raving mad. Already he held all of Europe and he had a non-aggression pact with Russia anyway. Leningrad was almost surrounded and the death toll was horrific. At least it would take some of the aeroplanes away from Britain and Germany would have too much on her hands to invade us. Then in July, the Americans occupied Iceland, taking over from Britain, who had held it since early in 1940. The Americans promised that they would give greater protection to the vital sea lanes for the convoys; so many of their ships were involved in bringing supplies to Britain now.

I signed off and took a week to go and see Sheila in London. She'd been bombed out again, so I gave her my new clothes coupons. I returned to Jarrow and signed on to the Pool in South Shields twelve days late. An elderly official reprimanded me and warned that if I continued flouting the regulations I would be in real trouble.

I said, 'It's all right you giving orders and sending me off, you don't know what it's like out there. You're safe.'

'I know what it's like,' he snapped. 'I was torpedoed twice in the last war and lost this leg.' He tapped his wooden calf and laughed. 'If you come across a half a leg, size nine shoe, that's probably mine.'

I said, 'Sorry. But just tell me what trouble I could get into that's worse than expecting to be blown up any minute?'

He didn't bother to reply to this self-pitying whine and prepared a travel warrant for me go to Middlesborough to join the Pool there. They sent me to the *S.S. Ashby*, owned by Ropener's. I was given a decent cash advance so I left an allotment for my father and drank the balance. Then next day I reported to Redcar Wharf.

The *Ashby* was a beaten up old tramp steamer that before the war had probably travelled the world picking up whatever charters she could find. There were several crewmembers from Sunderland including a big redheaded fellow called Anty Forrest who was fairly new to the service. He had been in the Army in Gibraltar and was bored to death there.

Some ship had been in port and was short-handed for its return to England. There were no seamen available in Gibraltar so they called for volunteers from the Army. Anty sailed on the ship to England. He'd only had about a week of sea-going experience but had been a coal miner at some time and was used to shovelling the black stuff. He was a strong heavy-set man, not too bright but a nice bloke. He would be our trimmer, while Joe Beck - a sixty-year old Dane who had lived in Sunderland for years - and I were the firemen on our watch.

We were a motley crew. One of us, a Londoner called Bannister, said, 'Call me Handrail.' I never knew what his first name really was. Then there was O'Toole, a little chirpy cockney from Stepney about forty years old and an old hand, and Williams, a Canadian from Halifax, Nova Scotia about my age.

The *Ashby* was still discharging the cargo of iron ore that she had picked up in West Africa. She was going to pick up another, which made the Sunderland men very uneasy. If a torpedo or mine hit a ship carrying iron ore, it went straight to the bottom like a stone. There were rarely any survivors.

The ship went up river to Middlesborough to bunker and take on ballast. When we were given shore leave, the Sunderland men said they were going home to see their folks. The ship was to go out on the 2:00 p.m. tide the next day, but they didn't show so three men from the Reserve Pool signed on at the last minute. These days there was no queue to jump on board ships though. Who would be stupid enough to volunteer for hell?

We did the customary trip up to Methil and round to Loch Ewe, where we had to wait for the convoy to assemble. The first few days at sea were unusually cold for October. After the Bay of Biscay, however, the weather warmed up and when we reached the Southern Atlantic we saw flying fish and dolphins. An enormous albatross followed the ship like the sign of good luck in *The Ancient Mariner*. All these new sights fascinated the first-trippers. Our convoy was well protected and even we old hands felt comparatively safe.

The trimmer on any watch had to go to the focs'le to wake the next watch, so this was Anty Forrest's job. He took such a long time to do this the first time that Joe and I got pissed off with him.

'It's that Handrail Bannister,' Anty explained. 'I can't wake the bastard up.'

I went to check this out. 'Call me Handrail' didn't just sleep; he went into a coma. We tweaked his nose, his toe, put water on his face and finally got him out of his trance. It took all of five minutes.

'If we're ever torpedoed, that bastard's got no chance in hell,' said Anty.

On a nice sunny day I was doing my 'dobying' on the poop deck, washing a couple of long-sleeved vests and my only pair of bell bottomed trousers. I was inordinately proud of them and thought I was Jack the Lad when I had them on. Anty was getting sun-tanned and the others were just loafing. A Scotsman, a first tripper who'd joined the ship as a trimmer at Methil, was telling me how much he was enjoying the trip. He'd worked as a coal miner in Kirkcaldy but had always dreamed of going to sea. He'd never been out of Scotland before and was really looking forward to it all. Then Williams the Canadian came up on deck. He was a nice lad but he was constantly using North American obscenities, which were not widely known in England at that time.

'That cook's a cock-sucker,' he announced in passing. The look on Anty's face was worthy of a photograph. He was a literal-minded chap

After a shocked pause, he said, 'Fancy that fucker saying that. I don't like the cook, but I'm sure he wouldn't do anything like that. I think he's a married man.'

The Cockney O'Toole winked at me. 'I don't know Anty. I heard someone call the cook a cunt.'

I provided the obligatory ending: 'Who called the cunt a cook?'

Suddenly the screw slowed, then picked up and slowed again. 'Sounds like trouble in the engine room,' said O'Toole.

'Christ, I hope we aren't going to fall out of the convoy,' I said.

But O'Toole was right. We had to stop for repairs. The convoy went on and a destroyer stayed with us for about six hours in the hope that we could fix the problem quickly. But when it became clear it was going to take longer, the destroyer signalled 'Good Luck' and sailed off to catch up the convoy.

The water was knee deep in the stokehole and the engineers worked all night. Early next morning they had completed the repair and pumped the water out. The rest of us had cleaned two boilers during the wait, so we got up a nice head of steam and started off again. It was 30th November 1941.

The old tub's top speed was only nine knots so it didn't seem likely that we'd catch up to the convoy. Joe and I were going on watch in ten minutes so we stood on the deck chatting. I was admiring my bell-bottoms flying in a nice breeze. They'd be nice and dry by now, I thought, I must remember to bring them in after our watch finished.

It was then that I told Joe Beck my ambition since the war began - to find a German and surrender to him. Then we went down to the stokehole, where I had a dirty fire to be cleaned. I pulled out the clinkers, Anty threw water on and I banked up the fire so the steam was holding well. I sat and poured myself a cup of tea from the growler, a big pot filled with tea so strong it could probably stand up by itself. I'd just got it to my lips when there was a terrific resounding crack. The ship gave a great lurch and the hot tea poured all over me. The boilers seemed to come out from their bedding and there was dust everywhere.

'Christ! That's a torpedo!' I shouted. 'Come on!'

I raced to the loose ladder and went up like a stampeding mountain goat. I was afraid it would break off, leaving us with no escape. I didn't want to drown in the stokehole. I could hear the other two thundering behind me, so I dashed up the next three stages. We'd started off in the very depths of the ship and must have come up those four ten-foot ladders in record time, terror lending wings to our feet. The ship was dying under us, with metal screaming and wood groaning as though it was in pain.

I felt my first sense of relief when we reached the deck amidships and smelled the fresh air. The torpedo had hit the stern, which had disappeared. Already the aft deck and hold were under water. The sea was only three feet below the side of the ship and coming up quickly.

Or the ship was going down.

'Hang on,' said Anty Forrest, 'I'm just going to get my photos.' He ran towards the focs'le.

He didn't come back.

Hang on be buggered, the water had reached our ankles. 'Come on Joe,' I said, 'We'd better get over the side.' I stepped over the handrail into the water.

Joe looked terrified; 'I can't swim.' His Danish accent seemed accentuated.

There was nothing I could do. We weren't wearing life belts because they made it impossible to shovel coal and in the panic of getting out we hadn't remembered them. I dropped into the sea and swam for my life. I knew I had to get as far as possible or I'd be taken down with the ship. I wasn't a good swimmer but now I thanked God for the hated lessons at school. When I had to pause to draw breath, I looked back. Joe had water up to his chest and hadn't moved. It was as though he was nailed to the deck. I swam a bit further and had to pause again; this time Joe had gone. The last part of the ship to sink was the poop deck where my pants were waving in the air. I remember having the irrational thought that my bell-bottoms had gone and wishing I hadn't washed them.

The poop disappeared and there was absolute silence for a few seconds as though the world had stopped. Then I became aware that I was being sucked into the whirlpool after the ship. Terrified,

I struck out again. I was still swimming but I was making no headway.

Then the boilers burst.

I was propelled away by the blast. There was a terrible pressure on my gut and balls and I yelled in pain. The explosion sent up debris and I watched it falling. Everything seemed to happen so slowly. A hatch cover came down and missed me by no more than a foot. I hung onto it in desperation.

I was exhausted but I had a profound feeling of relief and hope. I was alive.

When I'd recovered from the worst of the shock, I looked around. There was a big swell so I couldn't see much, but I could hear yells all around me. The hatch cover took me to the top of a wave and I almost burst into tears of relief to see a lifeboat in the water. It must have been launched from the other side of the ship. Had we known that, perhaps Joe could have been saved. I raised my voice to join the shouts of others who wanted picking up. I wished they'd all shut up so the lifeboat would come for me straight away. In the same trough that I was in I suddenly saw the Scotsman. He hadn't found anything to hold onto and was panicking, flailing about shouting, 'Mother save me! Mother save me!' I called out for him to swim to me, the cover would support two but he just carried on calling until his head went under the wave.

The lifeboat kept going in different directions and now bodies were drifting past. One wore a lifebelt but he was dead. He just kept bobbing.

The sound and sight of men dying is an awful thing to bear. I was crying, for him, for Joe and Anty, but mostly for myself. I started praying. Not the Act of Contrition Catholics usually make when their lives are at risk. I was asking God for redemption in this life. I didn't want to die. At this stage I felt an Act of Contrition would have been an admission of defeat. I was trying to make a deal that if He spared me I'd do better. I'd lead a good life, stop drinking and help my fellow man.

Every time I topped a swell, I saw the lifeboat about a hundred yards away. It would seem to be heading towards me but then it would sheer off to the left or right to pick up another survivor. I hated them. My deal with God had to go on hold. I had terrible thoughts like, 'I hope they don't see that bloke yelling. I hope they come for me first.' I can't claim to have felt any compassion for my fellow man when I was in such mortal danger. The sky was darkening; night would soon fall and perhaps they wouldn't be able to find me. Please God let them come soon.

After many detours and what seemed like hours, the boat finally came alongside and tired arms dragged me in. I lay in the bottom and let the world pass me by for some time. I had a sense of euphoria. I didn't care if I lay there forever. I was safe.

I just thanked God that I was a survivor. Up to now I'd never before accepted that I may be killed. In my stupid young arrogance I'd thought it only happened to ships I wasn't on. When I'd seen ships go down and men killed it was like seeing it on a movie. Even if I knew them. At last I realised that I was part of the target, not a witness.

From that day on, fear replaced arrogance.

Chapter 8
Lifeboat

The SS Ashby sank in two minutes. I don't know how so much could have happened in that time, but in memory the whole episode seems to float in a slow motion dream.

The lifeboat was in the sea because of the quick thinking of two deck hands from South Shields who'd taken one of the hatchets placed near each lifeboat and chopped away the davits at one end. That end of the boat fell straight down, tipping out many of the supplies. Then they chopped away the other end. By then the ship was almost level with the sea and the boat fell the remaining few feet into the water. It was fairly full of survivors by the time I got into it. The last two got in just in time; the sharks had arrived in a feeding frenzy.

The first mate was the only officer present and he took charge.

'The situation is this,' he said. 'We have water, pemmican and some concentrated chocolate, but we've lost the compass. I intend to drop sea anchor and wait. Hopefully, by daylight the weather will have calmed down. Then all being well, we'll set sail.'

It was dark now and he started studying the sky and stars, making notes by the light of a small torch. It was comforting to see him working; I felt quite safe in his hands.

I couldn't sleep because I was soaking in my dungarees and vest and I'd lost my shoes. My bare feet were in water to my ankles. There was no room to stretch out so we would have to sit up. The night had turned freezing cold with a chilling breeze. Stores such as blankets had gone overboard and we were lucky to have any food at all. We didn't get any rations that night though because the First Mate was too busy plotting our course by the stars.

We had counted the survivors and calculated the missing. I knew that Anty and Joe were definitely dead. Handrail too was lost; he probably didn't even wake up. Our watch engineer was gone, as was the chief engineer who had bobbed about in the lifebelt, dead. The Scotsman and O'Toole, the cockney, also. But Williams the Canadian was in the boat as well as a young lad called Harper, a year younger than I, and the fifteen-year old cabin boy. Humble, the cook had also survived but it was only a stay of execution for him as he would be lost on his next trip. Suffering from shock and some minor cuts, we numbered twenty-two. The ship's carpenter had lost a finger and was in pain. We had to pour on iodine, which was our only antiseptic. I think I cringed more than he did as it hit the open wound.

The radio operator was crying and yelling and we had to restrain him. He had plenty of excuse. He had stayed at his radio sending out distress call and our position; he was a very brave man and he went down with the ship. When the boilers exploded he was hurtled out and up onto the surface of the ocean. He wasn't physically hurt, but the shock had traumatised him. We huddled closer to make a space for him to lie down.

We were all so glad to have survived that we didn't even moan about cold or hunger. I just hugged my body and let my teeth chatter. The night eventually passed and at dawn the First Mate told us the situation.

'I'm going to try to hit the Azores by dead reckoning. They aren't very big in this ocean, and if we miss them it will be a thousand miles further to the coast of Africa. The SOS was sent giving our position and we may be picked up. I believe we will find the Azores'

That was good enough for me. Someone responsible was going to save me. I had absolute trust in him and it never wavered. The man was a natural survivor.

At 4.30am we put up the sail and pulled in the sea anchor. The First Mate set course and we had a fair wind. The seas were calming and –thank God- it was getting warmer. At last we had our first rations. Our water ration was as large as a medicine dose. The pemmican was the size of three postage stamps, the chocolate the same. The pemmican tasted vaguely of meat and was as hard as shoe leather. It took ages to chew a bite so it gave the illusion that we were having a long feed. The chocolate must have been stuffed full of vitamins; it bore some relationship to chocolate, but not a lot. The water was in a barrel and pincers held the tiny cup, which you immersed in a tiny plughole. When it came our turn we drank immediately so the cup could be passed on. We would get another meal in five hours.

I'd been accustomed in childhood to being very hungry. Sometimes I'd had no idea where the next bite was coming from, so I didn't suffer from the lack of food and water as many of the survivors. Instead, I found the sunburn most painful. There wasn't an inch of shade and the sun was merciless. I had either to let my body burn so as to shelter my face with my vest or expose my face to cover part of my body. As a result, every bit of me above the waist was blistered. Thank God I had my pants on.

But that first morning as the sun warmed the boat up, I began to feel quite cheery and I suddenly burst forth singing, 'A life on the ocean wave, alive on the ocean wave' The first mate looked around and for the first time grinned and nodded. This unaccustomed approval went to my head and I kept going. I presented my version of all three Inkspots singing 'Whispering Grass.' After a while they all joined in 'Hang out our washing on the Seigfried Line'. Even the Radio Operator's lips moved to that one. It broke through the shock we'd all been suffering and the men began talking normally.

'I suppose by now our people will know that we've been torpedoed,' a Geordie said. 'Our lass Kitty will be at her Ma's, crying her eyes out about me. "Oh, our poor Jimmy's gone!" she'll say. I couldn't get a kind word out of her last time I was home.'

His mate grunted, 'Aw no, she'll be with our Lizzie Ann in the Golden Lion having a good piss-up with the allotment money.'

A man had to hang his bum over the side to crap. The First mate said, 'It would be appreciated if all the shitting and peeing could go on well before we have our meagre meal.'

'And don't forget to wash your hands' someone shouted, 'it can be quite dangerous.'

I fell asleep in the sun and when I woke my ankles were already burnt. The constant spray from the sea cooled us, but eventually the salt cracked our skins. Night came and with it the freezing cold. Not quite as bad for me as the previous night because now my clothes were dry. I started to long for the next day and the burning sun. This was the pattern for every night and day.

In the morning a deckhand said, 'Hey, you know that quiz we used to play off watch? I've found the questions here in my pocket.'

'Great,' we said, 'that'd make a change'

The first question was, 'What year did Hughie Gallagher sign on for Newcastle United?'

The answers came thick and fast – all different.

'Come on then, tell us the answer, I know I'm right.'

The quizmaster's head was in his hands, his shoulders shaking. When he stopped laughing, he said, 'I only have the questions, I left the book with the answers on the mess room table.'

That didn't stop the argument. All speech, all animation was good. To sink into lethargy and despair was the danger.

Someone said, 'I lost my radio. I got it the last time I paid off. And I bought a lot of batteries too. Will I get compensation?'

The cook said, 'It wouldn't matter if you lost a thousand pounds or ten. All we get if we survive is thirteen pounds for loss of gear. If we don't survive we get fuck all. And our wives get the same. Nothing.'

Someone said, 'But we get our pay, don't we?'

'Will you hell, your pay stopped the minute we were torpedoed,' said the cook. That caused uproar.

He appealed to the First Mate. 'That's true, isn't it, sir?'

The mate reluctantly nodded agreement.

'Bugger me,' said another sailor, 'They can't do that. Look, SS Ashby is written on this lifeboat. We're still on company property.'

'They'll probably charge us rent for using it,' said the cook. 'There is some good news though. As the log, the records and the Captain – God Rest Him – have gone to the bottom of the sea, you won't have to pay for any slops you bought.'

A sad voice mourned, 'I've been saving up to get married and I didn't buy a thing.'

The fifteen-year-old cabin boy, Joe, looked as though he was regretting his career choice. More so when I said quietly, 'The sharks are back.'

We watched them in silence as they circled the boat, sleek and dangerous. I could see their eyes; they were too close for comfort.

'I wonder if we could catch one for food?' some smart bollocks asked.

'They're thinking exactly the same thing,' said the First Mate.

They went away after a while.

The carpenter was bearing his pain stoically. 'Look on the bright side, if we'd been hit after we loaded the bloody iron ore, we'd be at the bottom of the sea by now.'

We had a few rousing choruses of First World War songs that everybody knew the words to, then on to the hit of the year 'the White Cliffs of Dover.' I tried to turn it into a jolly little ditty but the favoured version was the mournful dirge of the Forces Sweetheart, Vera Lynn. More food, more idle chatter, doze in the sun, night, sleep.

I don't know how the others coped mentally, but I felt suspended in space and time.

The heat haze had faded the horizon line and we existed in a giant blue ball.

At one point we were singing:

> "When there isn't a girl about
> You're oh so lonely
> When there isn't a girl about
> You're on your owney.
> Absolutely on the shelf
> Nothing to do but play with yourself
> When there isn't a girl about."

My mind and body seemed to slip away. I had this vision of being up high, high in the limitless blue sky looking for the source of the noise. There was a pinprick-sized boat on the ocean, full of men roaring their lungs out, and no one to see or hear for hundreds of miles. There seemed to be only us in the whole world.

Except that soon there WAS other life. A ship! It was many miles away, but we shouted and yelled and waved our arms. There was no way we could be seen from that distance. Our deckhands set off flares, but either the ship's watch wasn't looking or the flares simply couldn't be seen in the strong sunlight. Sadly we watched it recede from view. Then around about two that afternoon someone thought they saw land. There on the horizon was something that looked exactly like a shoreline and it was on our direct course.

The First Mate looked doubtful and tried to restrain everyone's enthusiasm. 'I don't want to dash your hopes, but I think it must be cloud. I don't believe we're that close to land yet.'

We continued sailing towards it, but it changed shape and we had to swallow our disappointment, Later that afternoon we saw seagulls. That was a very good sign, because although they flew long distances they usually stayed within a hundred miles of land.

There was a lot of time for thinking and I did my share. It amazed me that the indoctrination of religion in my childhood was so deep-seated. I had rejected the whole concept of life after death-Virgin births, resurrection, Heaven and Hell – all at about the same time as I stopped believing in Santa Claus.

Now, sitting in the comparative safety of the boat, I couldn't believe how earnest my supplications had been when I was in the sea. When there was danger I prayed for my salvation. When the danger passed, I was again analysing the successful conditioning of my Catholic teaching. I would remain absolutely consistent in this inconsistent behaviour throughout my life. In any sort of crisis where a decision would affect my well being, I prayed. Once everything had turned out all right, I analysed and rejected the whole idea of a superior being. I was either an atheist or a supplicant for God's help. It reminded me of my Aunt Nellie Nee. Once when I was about fourteen she rose from prayer and caught my look of disbelief.

'Oh, well,' she said 'It's best to be on the safe side.' She was a pragmatic woman who had been heard to say, 'God is good, but the Devil's not too bad.'

When dawn came on the fifth day, we saw something in the distance that looked faintly like a church steeple. We sailed towards it all day but it seemed to come no closer. Night fell and the cold with it. Our rations had been cut the previous day as we were getting short of supplies; now we had fewer reserves to fight the cold.

However in the morning the steeple had turned into a cathedral, reaching miles up into the sky like a beacon of hope. We couldn't believe that any land came so far out of the sea, though we knew this time that it was land. Unfortunately it was still a long distance away when night fell again. It had been in view now for twenty-four hours already. We were cheerful though, for next day we'd be even closer.

Suddenly and dramatically in the black night a brightly lit ship was coming towards us. It had to be neutral to be showing lights. Light was an understatement; none of us had seen that much light since the war started.

It was like a magic ship gliding across the sea. I couldn't take my eyes away. We put up flares and the ship disappeared! They had turned off their lights. Blackness was blacker than it had been before, and so were our spirits.

'The rotten bastards, why did they do that?'

We found out later that it was a regular ferry service between the Azores, Madeira and Portugal. It was full of passengers, and the Captain was afraid of complications if he picked us up, for these were perilous times for all ships. Nevertheless, he had radioed our position ahead.

The next morning the cathedral-like mountain was in full view, but there was another island even closer that we headed for. As we approached, we saw high, sheer cliffs with giant waves smashing against them. It was a daunting sight, but to our surprise there were hundreds of people on top of the cliff waving to us. Two longboats, each manned by six men, came out from an invisible cove.

They were Portuguese fishermen, one of whom spoke English. 'Welcome, we've been expecting you. We can take three of you at a time. I will take the first three and then the other boat will come alongside for more. There is a very bad cliff you must climb.'

The radio operator and the carpenter were in the first boat. Both boats filled up, rowed to shore and returned for more.

'As we haven't any women and children, How about cowards first?' I suggested. However I had to wait for the fourth boatload. When we landed I saw the radio operator being hauled up the steep cliff by two men. He was tied to them both. They took him to hospital and we didn't see him again.

When the fisherman had said, 'bad cliff to climb' I'd assumed that he meant by an iron ladder or some similar contraption, but there were only hand holds on the rocks. Although it wasn't quite as sheer as it had looked from the sea, it was a formidable climb for men who'd had barely room to move for seven days. My feet were in bad condition from having been in water all that time, spongy and pitted. My legs were stiff and cramped the minute I straightened them. I had to stamp about on the shingle to restore circulation before I tackled the ascent.

I was as strong as a horse normally, but now my legs were shaking with weakness. My clothes had become so stiff with salt water that they chafed my skin with every movement. When I arrived breathlessly at the top I got an awful shock. The place was full of people shouting, clutching at me, hugging me and trying to pull my legs from under me to carry me. I realised that their intentions were kindly and welcoming, but this pulling about was frightening. I wasn't used to feeling physical weakness.

Movie cameramen were winding the handles of their cameras. Once I realised that everyone was friendly I began enjoying the attention, but I appreciated the hot drinks even more. It was strong black coffee, about strong enough to stand a spoon upright in.

We crossed the island by bus to a hotel, where they ushered us into a dining room that had long tables set out. They knew we were coming and had been preparing food for two days. The hunks of bread vanished as fast as a flock of seagulls could have demolished them. Waiters hurried in with tureens of soup and trays of fried eggs and bacon. The very smell of the food had us all salivating and groaning in anticipation.

I had read somewhere that starving people couldn't eat big meals. They couldn't have been talking about torpedoed seamen, because we ate everything in front of us. Never mind the order that civilised dining ordains. When the fried eggs appeared, I ate ten before the soup was ladled out. I didn't notice good manners prevailing anywhere at the table. Lots of coffee and jugs of wine, which were refilled time and again added to our happiness.

A wonderful feeling of bliss crept over me, no doubt fuelled by the wine. It was so nice being cosseted, eating hot food, and getting warm with people asking did I want more of anything. I never wanted to leave this lovely room and these wonderful people: it must all be a dream. I felt so safe I fell asleep with my head on the table.

Later the bus took us to a Portuguese destroyer called the Lima. The people of the Azores were wonderfully kind to us and we appreciated it. We were still wearing the clothes we'd been rescued in, which were as hard as boards.

Portuguese explorers and sailors have always been wonderful seamen and they really practice the fellowship of the sea; they collected every garment they could spare and got us all re-clothed. It added to my feeling of opulence to have something soft next to my body as well as inside it, even though I was dazed with exhaustion. The trip took only seven hours but we hadn't had a proper sleep for days apart from the odd catnap sitting up in the lifeboat.

The cathedral-like landmark was an island in the Azores called Pico, the highest point of which was 7713ft: no wonder we'd seen it so far away. The island we'd landed on was Faial, whose main town was Horta. The destroyer took us to Ponta Delgarda on the island of Sao Miguel. Here we immediately boarded the passenger liner Araggio Cavalho, which plied a regular passenger service between Lisbon, Madeira and the Azores. This was the very ship that had turned its lights off when we were in the lifeboat.

At last we got some proper sleep in bunks. We had the lowest deck with our own mess room and we slept four to a cabin. The food was fabulous, and the whole trip was so dreamlike that I can't remember how many days it took; my memory seems to focus entirely on the mess room. I do know that there was plenty of wine as it was a passenger ship. I slept, ate, drank, and then slept, ate drank again, in a state of bliss. I suppose I went up on deck, but I can't remember. I'd already seen enough sea to last me a long time.

We all managed to make it onto deck to see our ship go up the Tagus River towards Lisbon. First we saw little fishing villages, then Estoril with its grand buildings and Casino. The Portuguese passengers told us that there were more deposed Kings living in Estoril than anywhere else in the world at that time. Then we reached the Tower of Belem, which had welcomed returning Portuguese explorers home for five centuries. I too was dying to get my feet on land and take a long walk.

We docked at the quays near the Praca de Comercio, which we called Black Horse Square as there was a statue of a horse in the middle. About the size of Trafalgar Square, a magnificent mosaic floor made of little black and white two –inch square tiles that formed a pattern of waves covered the area. When a tile came up, a workman with a tiny hammer would come and tap a new one in place. I have returned many times since, but sadly the mosaic was eventually pulled up and replaced with tarmac. The demands of the automobile turned it into a car park, which is always extremely crowded.

The newspapers were there to greet us. They lined us up on deck for a group photograph, which appeared on the front page of the daily paper along with an article we of course couldn't understand. Two English officials came on board, and they mentioned that the Japanese had bombed Pearl Harbour and that the United States had entered the war. This meant nothing to me; no war was my war, and I felt the Yanks were well able to look after themselves.

More important to hear was the fact that the convoy we'd had to fall from had been attacked by U-boats and a number of ships had been sunk. As the carpenter had pointed out 'at least we were sunk before we loaded the iron ore.'

We'd been very lucky to survive. Life had become very precious to me.

The officials took us in a bus to a big pensao (boarding house) close to Black Horse Square. Next stop was a clothing store, where we were each fitted with a suit, three shirts, three vests, underpants, a spare pair of pants, socks, two pairs of shoes, and a pair of slippers. I had wanted a trilby hat all my life and I took this golden opportunity to get one. My word, I did look smart I thought.

I hoped I'd be able to keep these clothes out of the Jarrow pawnshops.

We were given escudos to the value of approximately two pounds and told we would receive the same amount from the British Embassy every Monday and Friday for the duration of our stay in Lisbon. We would also get our meals from the pensao. I didn't smoke so my money went a long way. Long may our stay last, I thought. My choice would be until the war ended.

In the end we were there for about four weeks and I enjoyed every minute of it. The tram system went everywhere very cheaply and I knew Lisbon inside out before we left. I also walked for miles through the old town, stopping at low class bodegas for wine. They were nearly all the same. An enormous barrel about ten feet high would fill a small room, leaving only enough space for wooden benches fitted as seats around the walls. We drinkers faced the barrel as if in obeisance to Bacchus. We hung on to our glasses and filled them from a spigot. I can't remember how much we paid but I remember it was incredibly cheap. My tongue turned purple from the wine. A pint of milk cost ten times as much; it was an alcoholic's Paradise. I hadn't yet become one but I got plenty of practice.

The Portuguese language was a mystery I couldn't unravel. From the Spanish I'd picked up so easily I could read the street signs, but the spoken tongue was incomprehensible to me. It seemed to consist of a lot of sounds like "sheesh" and "eeow".

Unfortunately the time came when they told us that we would leave the next day. We assumed that we were going home but we were wrong. We went unescorted on SS Harborough to Gibraltar, about a day's trip that passed without trouble. We stayed there for two weeks in the Seamen's Home. Gibraltar seemed entirely inhabited by men; the women and children had been evacuated to England when Italy came into the war. The very few who remained were the Spanish who worked in the big hotels. They went home across the border to La Linea each night, leaving behind the equivalent of a monastery.

We were brought up to date on the latest war news. The Japanese had not only bombed Pearl Harbour but had marched across the East. Where armoured carriers had been unable to go, they used pushbikes. They took Hong Kong on Christmas Day then 'impregnable' Singapore and all the islands down as far as New Guinea soon after.

Because of the dearth of females, the main occupation in Gibraltar was drinking and as a result fighting. I wasn't averse to these pastimes. I met up with an old acquaintance from Newcastle nicknamed Big Mac and we greeted each other like Stanley and Livingstone. He took me to his army barracks, where there was a very relaxed atmosphere. The poor bastard squaddies had been there a couple of years and were bored rigid. They even envied my recent adventure, silly sods; no wonder Anty Forrest had volunteered out. I spent about five days with them.

Mac was a wild man when he took a drink. One day we were in a bar and he suddenly went berserk, probably out of boredom. One entire wall was covered by a vast mirror and for absolutely no reason he picked up a chair and hurled it. The mirror crashed down, shattering shards of glass like bullets and probably bringing a thousand years bad luck. Within seconds the place was filled with military police, and Mac was carried off screaming and cursing. He disappeared off the Gibraltar scene after that.

It must have been about 1954 when I next saw him coming out of a bar in King's Cross. We had another Stanley and Livingstone meeting.

'Am I glad to see you,' he said, 'I haven't seen you since before the war.'

'What about the week we spent together in Gibraltar?' I asked.

He looked bewildered.

'When you were in the army,' I prompted. 'When you broke the mirror in the Universal Bar'.

'Jesus, I know I broke the mirror; I got six months detention. But I have absolutely no memory of seeing you there'.

'You can't remember anything?' I asked incredulously.

'I can remember six bloody months jail. I didn't have a drink and I got the D.T's'.

He must have spent a lot of his army life blacked out like that.

In another week, we were on our way home on a Polish troopship that had been a passenger liner in peacetime. All the ships that had been at sea when Poland was invaded had formed a fleet and become part of the Allied war effort. This ship was the SS Batori and it carried well over a thousand men as passengers – rescued sailors from several sunken ships and submarines, nationals from occupied countries who wanted to join their own country's armies based in England, and British troops. The most numerous living creatures, however, were the lice.

It was about twelve hours before they attacked me. I scratched a little itch; it didn't improve, so I removed my shirt. When I saw them I was nearly sick; I had a horror of such things. I took off my underclothes and used the limited facilities to wash them. It made no difference; these bastards weren't going to budge for a little soap and water. I can't remember anything about the actual journey on the Batori except that the lice caused me as much misery as the cold and heat on the Ashby's lifeboat had done.

At last we docked and were taken to the de-lousing centre. I had my hair cut down to the scalp. Then we stripped and I sadly watched my smart new clothes being consigned to a furnace. The loss of my trilby hat was the worst. We went through a steam bath and scrubbed with a bar of yellow sunlight soap. Then we received clothes from the seamen's mission. It felt like a re-birth, but they weren't like my stylish gear.

Everything had been organised. First we got an account of the wages due to us; mine wasn't much as I'd had an advance in Middlesborough and our trip had been cut short by six weeks. My net reward for the whole horrific experience was almost nil, except for memories that have never left me. I would have to rely on my 'loss of baggage' money to give me a few quid in my pocket. At least I got my rail warrant.

I didn't go for a drink with the others; I hadn't been alone for months. I wanted to get home, so I caught a train straight to Newcastle. I was early and got a window seat. The carriage quickly filled with six young ATS girls (Auxiliary Territorial Services) and a soldier who soon was talking to them and starting them giggling. I was still only twenty, so some of the girls were perhaps older than I. Certainly the soldier was, but even so I felt middle-aged and sad. I looked out the window and relived the past three months.

Faces of the dead came into my mind. It wasn't that they had been close friends, but these first violent war deaths had shocked and frightened me. I'd have to be stupid to think any longer that I was just a civilian spectator. The Merchant Service weren't even combatants, just prey, and bloody badly treated at that. I was seething at having endured that sort of trip and coming home with nothing in my pocket. I thought it appalling that our pay had stopped from the minute we were sunk. It made me angry. None of the wives and families of the dead men received any sort of compensation or pension either.

Soon I became aware of sideways glances from the uniformed gigglers and realised how I must look to them. I was young, tanned, fit. Why wasn't I in uniform? In the First World War they would have kept a little supply of white feathers to hand out. I looked at their complacent little faces and wondered how they thought the food arrived to fill their bellies, not to mention ammunition for their guns, petrol for the tanks and tinned food for their Mum's rations. Not one of them had seen as much as our fifteen-year-old cabin boy and probably never would. It was most fortunate for that soldier that he kept his mouth shut, at least to me. I was in the mood to smash someone up, and he was the most likely candidate. What could they do? Put me in jail? That would be a doddle. The idea of punching him in the nose grew in charm; fortunately the train pulled in to Newcastle and the great uniformed warrior got out amid girlish giggles.

I think it was about that time that I became an angry young man.

Chapter 9
SS Flowergate

I had only two days leave due, to which a survivor's quota of another five days was added. My money soon ran out, but not my anger.

I brooded about the money the ship owners were making from the derelict old tubs that had been rusting away in ships' graveyards. Now they filled them with goods and got our slave labour to man them. If the ships were sunk, they stopped the seamen's pay and put every penny of the insurance money into their own filthy mean pockets. The government obviously connived in this arrangement. We must be mad to take part in this exploitation. I knew that every man and boy who had ever gone to sea had been called back to man these rotten hulks. If they needed supplies so badly to win this war, why didn't they pay us properly?

Of course peacetime has dreadful traumatic experiences. Fires like King's Cross tube, Motorway accidents, earthquakes, bush-fires, hurricanes and all the other horrors that Nature can cause, apart from those that man can make for himself. But wartime terrors are different because for those in the front line it is the knowledge that the trauma will be repeated; that probably the same thing will happen again tonight or tomorrow.

Like the civilians in Britain who were living through the dreadful bombardments, civilian merchant seamen felt absolutely helpless because they had NOTHING to fight back with. No retaliation at all. I felt like a victim, and I didn't like the feeling.

Financially I could last only about three days, so I had to forego my remaining leave. On the 23rd January 1942, the Pool sent me to sign on with the SS Flowergate. In the Sunderland shipping office, I saw a big fellow from Jarrow who had been in the Merchant Service for many years; he was older than I, about thirty-six. I didn't know him very well but he recognised me and we palled up. We were the only two men from Jarrow; the rest were from South Shields and Sunderland.

North Shields was always called North Shields; it was across the Tyne River. South Shields was just called Shields. It was Shields and Jarrow that carried out rivalries.

'The Shields might cause a few problems,' I said to Sammy. 'Not for us,' said Sammy confidently.

He was probably right. I was 5ft 10ins and built like a heavyweight boxer, while Sammy at 6ft 2ins was an enormous man for those times when the average height for English males was 5ft 6ins.

We got large advance notes, which we wanted to cash. Officially speaking though, only a parent, wife or other designated person could do this, and then not until three days after sailing. As most seamen wanted an advance before they sailed, there were always money lenders who took 10%, as well as shops which would accept them for goods.

Pubs would do this too, if they knew you well enough. If you cashed the note and didn't get on the ship, the loser was the person who had cashed it. Sometimes seamen got drunk and missed their ship. If so, they would usually make a point of squaring the shortage, otherwise they would never get another note cashed in that town again.

Two Sunderland men were going to cash their advances and offered to introduce us to their man. He refused to oblige however, as he didn't know us. Then two other men who appeared to be seamen offered to take us to another cashier. They led us over to the other side of the river. At the end of a street, they stopped and said, 'it's just down there. If you give us the notes we'll take them in and get the money. We'll be back in ten minutes.'

I was speechless. Surely these little pricks didn't think we'd fall for that. Sammy turned to them, 'I've a good mind to smash your teeth in. You've walked us across that bridge, wasting our time. I might even kill you.' He made a movement toward one of them and they turned tail and scuttled like frightened rabbits. It was probably their regular con trick. We cashed the notes in Jarrow and had a few drinks with friends.

Sammy was engaged for nearly twenty years to a barmaid called Annie. He left his allotment with her every trip so she could save it for their future home. They were intending to marry at the end of every trip, but there was always a reason why the wedding had to be postponed. It was still going on. Many years earlier, Annie had said that she wouldn't marry him unless he converted to Catholicism, so he had received instruction and become Roman Catholic. Like so many converts, he was more passionate in his beliefs than most born members. Nothing ever shook his faith.

An American actor named Victor McClaglan played every Irishman in Hollywood- boxers, priests, union leaders and gangsters. If an Irish tough was required, Victor was their man. Sammy was not Irish, but he was McClaglan's double. He was also the most awkward man I ever met in my life. He fell over hatch covers and even up stairs, he dropped things and in general was a walking disaster. What a funny man he was though, and a wonderful shipmate in bad times. Thank God, he survived the war to become the Engineer on the ferry between Jarrow and Howdon.

The SS Flowergate took the usual route out of Sunderland up to Methil. But once we were at sea we were horrified to find that we had RATS. Every ship has them, but this ship had hundreds. They would get up on the mess table; they were absolutely unafraid of us. A small delegation went to the First Mate to complain. He took them to the Captain, who said he did know that there were a few rats and that he would get them destroyed in Methil. The previous crew had been Buddhists, who not only had refused to kill them but had actually fed them, so they became tame.

Nothing happened at Methil, so another delegation went to see him. It hadn't been possible – no time – it would be done in Loch Ewe. Once there we waited for a convoy; we were none too happy to hear that the Germans had started using subs in what they called Wolf Packs with at least eight to a pack. About the only good war news was that the Russians were taking advantage of the winter weather to push the Germans back. It must have been hell in that cold.

Once again though, nothing was done about the rats, which had extended their territory to the officer's quarters amidships, where they probably found better pickings. At least this made the bastards finally agitate for some action, but again nothing happened because we were too close to sailing.

One day we were watching the two soldiers wipe and polish their Bofors gun.. It reflected the light like a mirror.

'I wonder if they were called up, or if they were pre-war soldiers,' I said. I couldn't understand them spit and polishing like this when there was no senior Army officer aboard.
'I don't really understand anyone joining the army in peacetime with all those bloody orders.'

'I did', Sammy said gloomily. We went into the focs'le and he told us of his army career.

'My father was in the First World War.' began Sammy 'He was only 5'5", which wasn't unduly short in 1914, though it wasn't tall. For some reason he developed an incredible admiration for the Guards, but with his height he didn't have a chance of joining them. As I grew up and up, Dad was thrilled that I was showing such promise. At fourteen years old I was his height and at fifteen I was 5'8". He'd rub his hands and rejoice; I'd be able to join the Guards. What a uniform; it was wonderful. At eighteen I reached 6'2", and my father said 'Well, son. Are you going to join the Guards?'

Now it wasn't that I wanted to join the army but I didn't know what I did want to do. I was unemployed and there weren't many options. As he was so keen, I let my Dad lead me to the recruiting office. They must have needed men badly because I was accepted for the Irish Guards. Two days later I was shipped to the barracks at Purbright, Surrey. It was the first time in my life I'd been away from the Tyne area. I knew I was still in England because I hadn't crossed any water, but I thought the people were speaking a foreign tongue. On arrival we were met by a giant of a redheaded man with a massive bristling moustache. He stood a full head above me.

He greeted us with a roar. **"Ahhtrrhhh!"** *I looked at him in alarm. He came over, dipped his head at least eight inches to the level of my eyes and repeated* **"Ahhtrrhhh!!!"**
His face was scarlet and his eyes blazed with loathing. Who WAS this bloody man? I'd only met him five minutes ago, and already he hated me. This was the moment when I knew that I wouldn't realise my father's ambition.

Someone whispered, 'The sergeant Major was saying
"ATTENTION !"

So I straightened up before he could murder me. Then another
moustachioed maniac appeared and said I should have a haircut. I
said I'd had one two days ago to come here.

"Adttttuswck"!!" *he screamed.*

Hadn't he heard? I tried again, louder. "I just had a haircut."

When the sergeant recovered his powers of speech he snarled, **"You**
stupid dozy little man! Don't question my orders! I said haircut.
I mean haircut"

Of course he meant a head shave, right down to the bone. I'd been
here ten minutes now. How could I escape from this hell-hole full of
screaming hysterical giants.

  We spent the next few days being shouted at by anyone with
a rank above private. The other cadets more or less managed to
understand that a screeched **"Grrths trssts!"** *mean't 'Right' or*
perhaps even 'left turn' and "Hrpph! Hrpph!" repeated, meant 'At
the double'.

  After a few days I kind of understood the sound
and managed to turn with the others.

  Then the bastards threw a curly. The Sar-major gave a bit of
a talk in his foreign yell during which I caught something to do with
O'Grady, Murphy, Maloney, or some Irish name but I didn't know
them. I didn't have time to ask anyone what he'd said, before the
roaring started again. **"Grrths Trssts!" "Hrrpph! Hrrpph!**
Hrrpph! Hrrpph!" *Then came* **"O'Grady says 'Grrrths trssts!"**
I turned right but the squad turned left.

  The Sar-Mayor approached me. The gist of the words was
that I was a scurvy little bastard who was bloody useless. I was an
idiot.

His red moustache bristled. **"What are you?"**

"I'm an idiot Sar-Major"

"I can't hear you. What are you?"

"I'm an idiot Sar-major".

"I can't hear you. What are you?"

"I'm an idiot Sar-Major."

Thank Christ he stopped there, I'd have needed my balls surgically removed to go any higher. I felt like screaming, **"There's no fucking doubt about it! I'm an idiot!"**

Just being there proved that.

Apparently O'Grady saying to go somewhere meant exactly the opposite. How bloody stupid can the Army get? A sleepless night lay ahead of me, as I tried to remember exactly what O'Grady meant. Did it mean turn the opposite way or did it mean that WHATEVER order followed O'Grady meant the opposite.

I said my prayers.

Day –to-day survival became my total preoccupation. Even the other rookies thought that Sergeant Major Biggs picked especially on me, but as long as he left them alone that was okay by them. I didn't make even one friend as everyone was afraid my misfortune might rub off on them. I was the local leper. Of course I suppose I WAS a bit awkward. I sometimes stepped on the heels of the rookie in front and made him fall over. On sloping arms, I once smacked my rifle into the face of the recruit behind me and he needed four stitches. That time it was bloody O'Grady's fault. It was hard sometimes to keep in step and juggle a rifle about. The Sergeant Major said that if I was given a gun with bullets I'd probably decimate the Irish Guards. He didn't realise that he'd be the first to go. He was the first and only man I've ever been scared of, and hated, in my whole life.

The screaming never ceased; some bastard would shout you to bed and scream again for you to get up. Something all of us suffered from was spending bloody hours cleaning our boots until we could shave in the reflection. Then some sergeant would come along and say they were filthy and to do them again. I tried to become invisible- to scrunch myself up small-but the old yell to straighten those shoulders came. We rookies couldn't have a shit except in double time. **"Hupp, Hupp, Hupp!"** I prayed for just one kind word.

My father sent me a letter and a corporal brought it in, opened at the first page. He spread it in front of my eyes. *Dear Son, how are you enjoying army life – Hup hup!-* said the corporal and I answered "Yes Yes, I've read it corporal, I'm ready," and he took it away. That was all I ever read of that letter.

Then, when I thought nothing could get worse, I found it could. After the first week we were issued with the Guards uniform hat, which is like a bus conductor's cap but with a different peak. This visor, as they call it, comes right down over the eyes and almost touches the nose. Its purpose is to make sure that the man has to keep his head right back to be able to see anything. He cannot look at the ground. As you know I can be a little awkward at any time, but this cap virtually disabled me. Experience had taught me to not protest at anything, but this surely was wrong.

The Quartermaster pulled the peak even further down over my eyes and shouted **" RIGHT TURN, FORWARD MARCH!"** The first bit was easy, but then I had to work on instinct. I made it to the door, but there I stepped off into space and fell arse over tip down two invisible steps.

"Get up Get up Hup Hup"

Stupid man this sergeant. He held no terror for me any longer because I couldn't see him. I would have liked a white stick and a *guide dog. In the next few days if anything bigger than   a peanut lay on the floor I tripped over it. My knees were red raw from knocking into chairs and benches. One particular accident brought real punishment on my head. I think the sergeant wanted to see if any of his new squad* **could** *march in step. As a precaution, I was sent to the cookhouse to be out of the way. I had a fifty-six pound bag of potatoes and a bucket of water and I was peeling away. This was happiness; no cap, just me and the potatoes. When the bucket was full, I stood up to empty it, but my timing was unfortunate because a trainee cook was passing with a tureen of hot vegetable soup. Over it went on the floor with him close behind. As he fell, he kicked over the pail of wet peelings, which joined the soup. He lay amid this mess and looked up at me.*

"You bastard, you did that deliberately." He snarled.

Of course I denied it, I liked the job in the kitchen and would happily have stayed there; no one can yell much about potatoes But now I was punished by having to run around the bloody parade ground carrying a hundred pound kit-bag on my back for hours.

Eventually this twelve weeks passed, but instead of being given a uniform, I was called into the Adjutant's office. "I'm sorry" he said, "but you aren't the material to make a guardsman."

I was confused. I didn't know how they would punish me, whether they'd shoot me or if I'd just get a flogging from the Sergeant Major.

'Here is your discharge from the Irish Guards.'

He handed me my piece of paper to freedom. It said **"Unable to fulfil the requirements of a guardsman."**

I was issued with a suit made of some material just slightly better than workhouse suits, which were made of hessian. Returned was a case with my own stuff that I'd worn on arrival. Two big guardsmen quick-marched me to the barracks gate. One noticed the tears on my face and said sympathetically, "Never mind, maybe you can join another regiment,"

'I'm crying with joy,' I told him.

I arrived home and my mother opened the door. She didn't look at all surprised by my appearance. 'Hello Sammy pet.' She shouted up the stairs, 'Dad! Our Sammy's come home.'

'Just a moment son while I put my trousers on.' he called. 'I'll come straight down to see you in your uniform'.

When my dad came down I was standing in this bloody awful suit, fifteen pounds lighter. Judging by the shock on his face I must have looked like a graduate from the workhouse.

'Where's your uniform?'

'They threw me out.'

The disappointment on the old man's face should have been heartbreaking, but I didn't care. I'd made the supreme sacrifice, and the twelve weeks had nearly crucified me. I became a merchant seaman as soon as I could, before the old man started dreaming up the Household Cavalry or somewhere else with a fancy uniform.'

We'd all had a great, light-hearted hour, but now the convoy was getting under way. Two days out we heard that we were headed for Philadelphia. I was thrilled; at last I would see something of the United States.

Now, with all of Europe's manufacturing capacity at their command, the Germans were making many more submarines. There were dozens of Wolf Packs. Our Sunderland flying boats were a good deterrent though, and had a range of about four hundred miles. They could bomb U-boats on the surface and drop depth charges if they were under the water. After some success by the Sunderlands the Wolf Packs move out of range. Then when they found a convoy, they would radio their position to other German subs which would then come to meet them. They couldn't move very quickly but sheer numbers meant that there were always some fairly close. The first Wolf Pack shot and torpedoed a convoy when they saw an opening before going home to re-arm. The second relay of subs would arrive and repeat the exercise. Now that there were so many they didn't save their ammunition for loaded vessels; it was just as good to sink the empty boats on the way out because they take a long time to replace. The Germans just wanted to stop supplies getting to Britain.

They located us about two days out and from then on we had very little sleep. I didn't think that anyone in the world would be more scared than I, but Sammy was. It was his vivid imagination that got to him. He'd been in convoys that had lost ships, but whatever ship he was on was never attacked. He lay in his bunk jerking at the sound of every depth charge and every roll of the ship. He prayed a lot, making an Act of Contrition every morning and night. Thereby ensuring his entry into the Kingdom of Heaven. I laughed at him, but he took it all very seriously and perhaps it was some comfort. As for me, I was shit scared. I was always aware of all that water beneath us. And when depth charges were dropped it was like living inside an enormous drum; we couldn't hear anyone speak.

And we had the rats to contend with. I was afraid that as we weren't feeding them they would eat us instead. I'd lie in my bunk watching as they sat on the mess table and cleaned their whiskers, just like bloody cats. I was always expecting one to drop in on me for a nibble.

At one time we went for two days without a sub attack, but our imagination kept making us think we'd be blown up without notice. We knew they were on their way, and the waiting was nearly as bad as an attack. Down in the stokehole I shovelled as fast as I could to get the hell to the U.S. as soon as possible. However we lost only two ships on that outward trip. It was a nightmare between rats and subs and I was very relieved to reach the Delaware River.

The ship was going to be fumigated, so we seamen were put in a comfortable hotel.

'I'm going up to New York to see the Shaughnessys,' announced Sammy. 'Do you want to come?'

'Of course I do.' I answered.

'We'll stay in this nice comfortable hotel until the rats are gone,' said Sammy, 'and then when they move us back to the ship, we'll go to New York.'

We went up to the centre of Philadelphia. I remember thinking it was funny that every street was named after a tree – Walnut, Pine, Oak, etc. I saw my first television set in a bar. A man was singing 'Seven years with the Wrong Woman.' Then a black guitar player took up the theme in the bar. Some drunk told me that he'd had twenty-seven years with the wrong woman and started bothering the guitarist to 'play the blues'.

'I am playing the blues,' the musician protested and broke into 'My Mamma Done Tole Me'

'That's the blues,' said the drunk.

I also saw my first teabag. I thought it was just a cup of boiling water with a string, so I complained to the waitress.

She said, 'Well gee, honey, we don't get much call for this stuff.' She showed me how to jiggle the bag to make the water darken. It was so horrible I never would have believed that teabags would take hold in England.

When we went back to the Flowergate the fumigators were packing up. The rats had been killed and were lying in five heaps, each the size of a bale of hay. There were hundreds of them, sleek and fat with shiny coats. Thank God they were dead.

One idiot snivelled that a ship without rats was unlucky. Sammy said, 'Don't worry, there are plenty left – they come from Shields.'

This was a foolhardy remark as we were truly outnumbered on the ship. We added insult to that particular injury by going off to New York without doing our cleaning job on the boilers. Sod them!

Sammy had been to New York dozens of times so I was glad to have an experienced guide who was such good company. The Shaughnessys were a large Jarrow family. The grandmother, her elderly sister, her son Johnny and daughter Julia lived in a brownstone apartment house on 106th Street. Nearby lived another married daughter named Mary. We were pleased to see that Pat Shaughnessy was there. He and I gone to the same school, but he was three years younger; I didn't know him all that well, but we were all part of the great Jarrow family. He'd come over on a ship eight months earlier that had docked in Baltimore. The family had driven all the way down there to bring him back to stay with his Granny for a while, so he jumped ship. Now he was seventeen, and already he'd grown into a big man. His hands were like plates, and he was exceptionally strong. He was also very good-looking, with the typical blue eyes and black curly hair of so many Irish. More important to Sammy and me, he had a great sense of humour and a total irreverence for authority.

The apartment was well situated, just half a block from a famous Irish bar called Feeneys. St Patrick's Day was coming up, and the city was getting decorated for the occasion. On St Patrick's Day we went to Fifth Avenue of course. A flower-covered float represented every county of Ireland with beautiful young girls adding to the spectacle. The mounted police went by, followed by hundreds of marching cops. Many seemed to be enormous fellows, though Pat, Sammy and I were no short arses. Sammy wore his inevitable cap, but this time it was green. His face was like an Irish potato, and as each new group passed he would raise his cap. The leader would respond with a salute and a great big grin. Marching girls in brightly coloured short skirts formed dancing patterns and dozens of noisy bands passed by. That night we went to Times Square to celebrate then back to Feeney's bar. Just as well it was only a few houses away from the floor of old Mrs Shaughnessy, where she'd laid out mattresses for us. Somehow we managed to crawl back.

Sammy and Pat took me all over Manhattan. We went to The Radio City cinema where the famous Rockettes danced in precision, not an inch between the height of their kicks. Johnny gave us a plug of tobacco for our fathers' pipes.

'And a bit extra to make some money.' he said.

In spite of this we had to return to the Flowergate eventually because we'd run out of cash. We didn't know or care if she'd still be in port, but she was. All the Shields black crowd had taken a day without leave, and they arrived back at the same time as we did.

'You're in trouble,' the engineer said, 'You'll be logged and lose your wages.'

'You're going to get hell,' the Shields mob jeered. We didn't care though, whatever the punishment it had been worth it.

The First Mate said, 'The Skipper will see you later, all of you. We have to pull out now.'

This the ship did, only to stop after thirty minutes to drop anchor in the middle of the Delaware River. We were puzzled, but the Captain sent for us before we found out what was going on.

There were Sammy and me, and three Shields lads. The Captain said,' You've taken leave without permission. I'm docking you a day's pay and fining you another day.'

A Shields man said, 'Are they going to get the same as us Sir? That's not fair, they were away for a week, and we had to do their cleaning. Why do we get the same punishment?'

The Captain started saying, 'Are you quest--?' when Sammy said, 'Shut your bloody face, you moaning bastard.'

The Shields man stepped forward to throw a punch at Sammy, but Sammy got in first with a haymaker.

Unfortunately, the skipper had wanted to finish his sentence and was purple with fury. He stepped forward, logbook in hand, only to have his chin connect with Sammy's punch. He was a tall man and he went down like a felled tree.

The Shields man was unable to pull up, and he tripped over the Captain. Sammy fell on top of both of them. Then a second Shields man took up the fight. As Sammy was on top I thought that Shields Two would kick him, so I floored him with a punch to the jaw.

Four down and two upright. I turned to Shields Three, who lifted his appalled gaze from the floor, to my face, and shot out the door.

Officers, stewards and deckhands filled the doorway. Shields Two managed to rise, allowing Sammy to get up. Shields One was in real bother though. He had to put a hand either side of the skipper's head to get leverage, and so the commanding officer's first conscious sight was Shield One's face just inches away from him, his body on top. The Captain was a big strong bloke in his forties, but he looked dazed.

'Get off me!' he roared and was helped to his feet by an officer.

'ATTENTION!' he shouted at the poor bloody Shields man. 'Right, you'll pay for this. This is practically mutiny. I'll teach you to hit me. You questioned my judgement, you interrupted me, and you went AWOL. You're nothing but trouble. I'M GOING TO THROW THE BOOK AT YOU!'

Shields One protested. 'I didn't, sir. It wasn't my fault. Nobody assaulted you, it was an accident.'

'Then whose fault was it?' Who punched me?'

Like twins Sammy and I pointed to Shields One and said, 'He did.'

The officers tried to find out what had happened, but the captain said he would deal with it later and dismissed everybody. When the time came--much later—the Shields man, whose name was Joe Jordan, was only fined one extra day's pay. We heard no more about the episode.

The Captain looked distracted, and I wondered if he had concussion; he didn't seem to have his heart in the job. The explanation wasn't long in coming though. A launch arrived alongside carrying about thirty men and two armed guards, all dressed in white rubber suits, heavy white rubber boots and head coverings with inset goggles and gloves. Astronaut suits before we'd heard of Astronauts. They put up notices: "No Smoking" "No Causing Sparks" "Must Wear Soft Soled Shoes."

One hold had been left empty. 'What the fuck is this all about?' we were asking. Then came the answer, pulled gently by barges. The hold was to be filled with ammunition.

Sammy let out a low moan when he realised what was coming aboard. 'Oh my God, why didn't we stay in New York for another couple of days, even eight hours? We'd have missed all this.'

I looked for a way to get ashore, but we were right out in the river. That's why they'd pulled us out there, so only one ship would be blown up if there was an accident loading. And the guards with guns were to keep us on the bloody ship. Sammy was having a bit of a problem coming to terms with the fact that his omnipotent God had left him in these dire straits. I sent up a few supplications myself.

Eventually the astronauts got off, and we headed out to sea where we sailed to Nova Scotia, unescorted by armed ships and unaccompanied by any other cargo ships. For the first two days we were as nervous as cats. All except Joe Jordan, who would do his watch, wash, eat his meal, and turn in. He'd sleep peacefully with no bad dreams and no movement except for his snoring. The man must have had nerves of steel.

Twitching away in his bunk, Sammy would stare at him, his hatred fuelled by every snore. 'Look at that bastard sleep,' he would say, 'I haven't had a minute since we left New York. Just listen to him.'

We had a little man, a Londoner I believe, who said, 'If we get hit with this lot, we'll go up like a matchbox. Flash, Puff, Finish'

To hear this once was bad enough, but he said it at breakfast, in the heads, anywhere. Always the same sentence. I was already well aware that the Ashby had gone down in two minutes. Less than that I didn't want to hear about.

'If we get hit by this lot, we'll go up like a matchbox. Flash, Puff, Finish.'

It was useless trying to read or play cards to get your mind off this. Sammy would flinch every time the Cockney repeated it.

One day we were lying in our bunks, very quietly and it started again, 'If we get hit…'

Sammy jumped from his bunk, went over and grabbed the Cockney by his throat. 'Flash, Puff, Finish. If you fucking say that once more on this ship, I'll make sure that you are fucking Flash, Puff, Finished. I'll choke the fucking life out of you.'

Sammy was trembling with exhaustion and anger, and the little guy's eyes were popping out of his head. He was terrified. No one bothered to restrain Sammy from his near homicidal attack, even the Shields mob looked approving.

He flung the Cockney back on his bed like a sack of potatoes. 'I'll fucking Flash, Puff your box of matches.'

Not one man ever mentioned the dangerous cargo again.

Chapter 10
Return on SS Flowergate

We arrived without incident at Halifax and joined a very large convoy of British, American, Canadian and European vessels. The ships were in lines, with most of the escorts on the outside and the minesweepers up ahead.

Two days out, at about 11.45 am. I was in the stokehole when the siren went off, announcing that U-boats were about. There was a terrific noise. Depth charges were being dropped and Action Stations were called. My watch finished in ten minutes and we went up on deck, passing the relieving twelve to four watch who said, 'Something is happening up there, buggered if we know what it is.'

The alarm went again, and suddenly I realised to my horror that the submarines had got past the destroyers and were running wild inside the convoy. These were new and different tactics. They skimmed across the surface between the lines of merchantmen; it was like being a lamb in a flock where wolves were running loose. They raced between the lines shooting their guns from both sides and firing torpedoes. It seemed like a suicide mission, but the destroyers couldn't fire into the middle of the convoy. They would have blown us up. The merchant ships weren't able to use their guns either, for the same reason. Our gun wasn't fired at all. Ships started sinking and others were burning. It was chaos.

The merchant seamen were thoroughly demoralised; we were at the mercy of the subs and all those destroyers and battleships couldn't help us. Now the reckless subs had somehow to dive and get out and away from the convoy. We saw pools of oil and debris several times and I think many of them perished. One of them surfaced too soon for its own good, in front of a merchantman, slightly to the port side. The merchant ship changed course, went Full Steam Ahead and rammed the sub, which disintegrated. A cheer went up.

Thank God the *Flowergate* wasn't attacked.

This episode felt like several weeks out of my life, but actually it finished at 12.10 p.m. Eight ships were sunk in fifteen minutes at the most. Nor was this the end of it--the other Wolf Packs out there knew our position and just had to bide their time. From then on we had no respite. Ships would be torpedoed in the middle of the night and the sirens would sound at least a dozen times a day. Everybody was exhausted and thoroughly demoralised; we never got a rest.

I had fully expected retaliation from the Shields men for the incident in the Captain's cabin, but nothing happened. One of them, Joe Jordan, wouldn't even meet my eyes. I was surprised because he was known for being a bit of a fighter.

I said to Sammy, 'That Joe Jordan must be even more frightened than I am. I thought I'd have to fight him, but he won't even look at me.'

Sammy said, 'Really, that's weird isn't it? If you keep looking at him, he'll have to see you eventually.'

The next day Sammy said, 'Joe Jordan doesn't seem to be sleeping so well, thank God. He used to drive me mad with all that snoring.'

I was confused by this sudden about-turn, but relieved. Those nights, we all lay on our bunks, sleepless much of the time. We never knew when hell would break loose again. I often looked across at Joe, remembering his calm for the first few days of the trip. The

Shields men had all stopped making dirty cracks, and I enjoyed the peace of it. I only had to fret about being killed by the Germans now.

The attacks went on intermittently for five days, but it was nothing like that first day and only one more ship was sunk. As far as I know, the packs were never able to break through a convoy in that way again, because the element of surprise had passed. The Flowergate came through unscathed, if that word applies to a crew on the edge of a nervous breakdown. But life returned to something like normal and we set course for home, joining a convoy coming from Loch Ewe on its way down the East Coast of England. There was a violent storm for the last three days of our trip, which normally would have been very frightening but as it almost stopped the movement of the subs, it seemed fairly benign.

We docked in Hull on the Humber River. Our trip had been four months in all and we paid off on the 21st May 1942. The usual gang came aboard--Health, Immigration, and Customs. We'd left our plug tobacco hidden and the Customs man put a white cross on the cases and kitbags, announcing that they had passed scrutiny. Then we threw away our old clothes, packed the tobacco in tightly, and walked off the ship thinking how clever we were. We laughed all the way to the bus stop opposite the dock gates.

Suddenly a dark car pulled up next to us, and three official-looking civilians dressed in dark suits got out. 'Customs and Excise,' they announced.

Sammy said, 'But our things have passed customs already, there's the mark.'

The senior man said, 'Yeah, we know that old trick. Open them up.'

Of course they found the tobacco. A junior man said, 'I thought as much, sir.'

'We're going to confiscate this contraband,' said the senior officer. 'We're not going to charge you as we hear you've had a bad enough time.'

They drove off. 'Why do I have the feeling we've been tricked?' I asked. 'We didn't see any papers or identification. They could have been crooks.'

Sammy said, 'I don't give a bollocks if they were crooks or Customs who now have a nice couple of months smoking ahead of them. We weren't in a position to antagonise them and finish up in the jail here. I want to go home and get married.'

We'd had a good payday, so I thought I'd better get a suit just in case Sammy did manage to tie the knot. He'd asked me to be his best man, saying he would definitely get married this time. I'd agreed, although I was fairly certain the wedding would never take place. A couple of Russian Jewish tailors had left cards in the pub promising to make nice suits at reasonable prices, so I had my first made-to-measure suit; what's more it didn't have to be cut to austerity standards, as I had plenty of coupons. It was very smart.

In retrospect, I realise that the highlights of my young life seem to be getting new clothes. It must have been because of my deprived childhood. My adulthood was deprived too, though, and I couldn't be sure this suit wouldn't finish up in the pawn like everything else.

We were having a drink at the station and reading the paper while we waited for a train to Jarrow. We'd heard a little about the Japanese advance in the Pacific and the whole situation sounded bad. The Americans had managed to attack Tokyo with bombers flying 600 miles from the Aircraft Carrier Hornet, and huge sea battles were being fought in the Pacific Ocean.

More important to us, however, was a cartoon in the Daily Mirror. The Mirror was doing everything it could to help merchant seamen get a fair deal. They had previously published the poem that appears in the preface of this book. Now the Government warned them that the paper would be suppressed unless it behaved. Herbert Morrison told MP's that the newspaper had repeatedly published scurrilous misrepresentations, with reckless indifference to the National Interest. He had reminded The Daily Mirror that it could be shut down under wartime Defence Regulations. Its latest offence was publishing this cartoon showing a distressed seaman on a raft over the words *"The price of petrol has increased by one penny."* Most MP's considered that this caption was intended to suggest that seamen are having to risk their lives to boost oil company profits. Winston Churchill "resented such criticism of the war effort."

"The poem, by Alfred Benjamin of Newfoundland was published under "He speaks though he is dead" on Friday August 15th 1941. His ship was bombed off our coast – and he was killed. A friend who was at his side when he died brought this poem to the Daily Mirror.

We print it because it shows how a Merchant Serviceman felt about the neglect which the public shows towards him and his mates.

He died doing the things he talks of in his poem. Can you read it - and still think so little and so seldom of these brave men?"

The Daily Mirror had done its utmost to help Merchant seamen.

"The price of petrol has increased by one penny" _ Official.

I said to Sammy, 'Now it's over, I really wonder what happened to Joe Jordan. I didn't think he'd lose his bottle like that. It was almost as though he was frightened of me. I'm not absolutely sure I could beat him in a fight.'

Sammy said, 'Well, I did tell one of the Sunderland men that you'd been in the loony asylum for a while, and that you carried a cut-throat razor around with you. I said you were particularly pissed off at Jordan and perhaps the Sunderland bloke should tell Joe to keep an eye open. I said I was afraid you might cut his throat.'

I laughed, 'What in the name of God did you say that for?'

Sammy was quite proud of himself. 'Well, I didn't want any aggro on the way home and I was pissed off at Joe. I hated him. You know how the bastard could sleep; nothing seemed to frighten him and I was scared every minute. It wasn't fair. I wanted to stop him snoring--it worked didn't it?'

About two years later I met an old schoolmate, Peter Kane. We had a drink and he asked me, 'Were you with a bloke called Joe Jordan on the Flowergate in 1942?'

'Yes, why?'

'Well, I was drinking with him one day. He started talking about Jarrow men and he called them 'Linskey's Bastards.' He said he'd spent the most terrifying trip of his life on that ship. On the way out, they had rats and that going home he had you - fresh out of a lunatic asylum and carrying a razor. He said the bloody bombs were bursting, but all he could do was watch you. You spent the whole trip staring at him. He was convinced you'd cut his throat if he fell asleep. You haven't been in a lunatic asylum, have you?'

I smiled, 'Not that I can remember.'

Now, Sammy and I finished our drinks and headed towards the train. I saw many uniforms I'd never noticed before, not necessarily service uniforms, although they all had peaked caps. The first was the ticket collector, who looked at our tickets as though they weren't valid, then looked at us, and decided to pass us through. Once on the platform, we saw other passengers being herded along by a peaked-hat porter. Two policemen approached; one of them was an auxiliary.

"Show your identity cards. Where are you going?'

'To Jarrow.'

'What's your name?' they asked Sammy.

'Samuel Cazeley.'

'How do you spell it?'

'For Christ's sake, can't you bastards read? It's right there.'

'Where have you come from?'

'We've come off a ship called the Flowergate that just got in from America. It was loaded with general cargo and enough explosives to blow Hull off the map.

Sammy pointed at me. 'And before that, he was in the lunatic asylum. I think that's where we're all going.'

Their faces whitened and the policeman pointed to the sign that read, 'Careless talk costs Lives.'

'There's a war on you know,' said the auxiliary.

'You don't have to tell us. We've just come from the fucking thing.'

These auxiliaries were Special Constables, usually older men who assisted the police in wartime and were always accompanied by a real police officer. All the coppers were on foot and still carried gas masks, which civilians had long ago discarded. There were also Auxiliary Firemen, Air Raid Wardens, Land Army, W.V.S., Demolition Squads, St Johns Ambulance Men, and Bus Inspectors, all in important looking uniforms. The whole country seemed in a state of siege, with signs everywhere like 'Careless talk costs lives,' 'Lend to Defend the Right to be Free.' and 'Dig for Victory.'
The train was filling but one carriage was empty. The porter bustled up.

'You can't go in there. It's reserved for members of the Spitfire fund.'

'Who the hell are they?'

'They're collecting money to pay for a Spitfire.'

'They certainly deserve a seat,' said Sammy, but of course the irony was wasted. 'We'll go next door.'

The carriage doors were locked at both ends, however, and no one could get through except the guards. So we stood in the corridor all the way to Newcastle. At one point the end door opened, and the porter came through with a tray holding a big pot of tea, cups, saucers, milk and biscuits.

'Just the job. We'll have a cup, please' I said.

'They're for the Spitfire people.'

At Newcastle we put our kits into the Left Luggage and went to the canteen for a meal.

'Spam and chips, please,' I told the waitress.

'You can have chips but there's no spam left.'

'Did the Spitfire Fund eat it all?'

She looked puzzled. 'No, there were twenty Home Guards in. They had it all.'

'Greedy old bastards,' I muttered.

We had the chips and a cup of tea. 'Do you think we dare go for a beer?' I suggested.

On the way to the pub, we were pulled up by the Military Police. Sammy was getting weary. 'Christ Almighty, aren't there enough civilian police without you bastards?'

'Don't call me that, address me as Corporal.'

'And you'll call me Sergeant,' said the other.

'We'll call you Bollocks,' I said.

'We can arrest you.'

'I wish you bloody well would. I'd get the first sleep I've had for weeks.'

Sammy said, 'For God's sake, Bill, let's show them our identity cards, or we'll never get away.'

They looked chastened when they looked at our cards. 'Sorry,' they said, 'But if you're not in uniform, you could be deserters.'

When we got back to Jarrow, Sammy went to the arms of his beloved. I didn't think there would ever be a wedding, though, because the romance had been on for too long already and must have gone off the boil by now. I went round to his house after a day or so.

'There's been a bit of a hitch,' he said. 'Annie's mum is ill, so we'll have to put the wedding off for now. It's a pity-Annie was keen to get married this trip.'

A couple of years later, Annie's final excuse was the most successful. She died. What's more, she hadn't left a will, and so her oldest sister inherited the money Sammy had been giving Annie for the last twenty years. He would see the sister's husband, a hard drinker, unsteadily returning home. 'There goes a skinful of my savings,' he would mutter resentfully.

I had only four days leave. The trouble with being sent back to sea so quickly was that our minds never had time to recover. The happy days of youth when heads just had to hit a pillow to sleep had passed forever. I would get to bed and lie in the darkness with rotten memories flying through my brain. By about the third night, I'd get a few hours sleep, but on the fourth I was anticipating whatever new hell would be launched on the next trip. I was nearly as mad as Joe Jordan had believed me to be. I was drinking a lot too, because that seemed to help some. At one time I used to spend my money mostly buying my father and friends drinks, but now they had to pay their share.

Petty Officialdom ruled in Jarrow too. Everywhere, I saw uniformed people who'd been pre-war deadbeats. Once they donned their outfit, they were under the impression they'd moved up a notch in the English class system and deserved to be seen as leaders of men. One fellow who used to sell newspapers in Jarrow was now an ARP Officer. If you opened the pub door in order to leave, it was,

'Shut that door, douse that light, stop that noise, don't do this, do that.' Every bastard in England was giving orders. I was stopped at least three times every day. On the third day I was so fed up, I pulled out my identity card and forced a pair of policemen to look at it.

'But we know you, Bill; my lad went to school with you.'

'That doesn't matter. Don't you know there's a war on?'

The peaked caps avoided me after that.

There were some lighter moments, though. The best laugh I had was in our neighbour Mrs Higgins's wash house, which she used when there was an air raid--she didn't have an Anderson shelter. It had less protection than her house, but it was outside so she thought it safer. I'd been chatting to her and a few of the women doing their weekly wash, and we all piled in there when the siren went. I remarked on its lack of protection.

One woman said, 'My Alf says that if one of them bombs has got your name on, it'll get you.'

'Jesus, Mary, and Joseph,' said Mrs Higgins. 'The things they do these days. Those bastards are clever, aren't they? I do hope they haven't written 'Mrs Higgins' on one of them.

Chapter 11

SS Amberton

When I went to the Pool to sign on, I found that things had changed. Bureaucracy had gone mad. I wished we were back in the days of making a pier-head jump.

Clerk: 'Go over to the Union Office to make sure you've paid your dues. They'll give you a green card.'

Linskey: 'Here's my book. You can see I've paid up for six months.'

Clerk: 'That doesn't matter; you'll still have to get your green card. It has to be official.'

I went off, grumbling that I didn't even want to be in the Union. What sort of a Union for seamen was it that was run by Lord bloody Yates? He was probably a Freemason, a bastard who'd never been to sea in his life.

At the union headquarters the clerk agreed I had paid up and gave me a green card for which I signed. I returned to the Pool.

Clerk: 'Now you have to go to the Seamen's Federation and fill in buff form, no. 256.'

Linskey: 'Christ, with a bit of luck I'll never get to sea if this goes on.'

The Federation had at least six more clerks than the last time I signed on. They all shuffled papers and looked vitally important to the war effort. One, whose uniform an Admiral would have envied, probably threw ropes onto the ferry before the war. By now I had no idea what I was doing, but I filled in about six more forms before returning to the Pool and signing on for the next available ship.

I said to the Pool clerk, 'The easiest part these days is shovelling the bloody coal and risking your life.'

'You aren't the first one to say that,' he said. 'We've got a job today if you want it. The *Amberton* is signing on crew at 2:00 p.m.'

I still had a day's leave, but I wanted the advance money.

Clerk: 'You have to go to the Shipping Federation.' He gave me a form to take and another little ticket. 'Then go to the Board of Trade at 2:00 PM.'

The shipping master signed me on, together with a number of others from Jarrow and North and South Shields. We were all for the Black crowd, firemen and engine room crew.

'Report tomorrow at 10:00 am to North Shields. The ship is in the Staithes, bunkering.'
That was where I'd got my first jump into the Merchant Service. It seemed a lifetime ago.

The *SS Amberton* belonged to a company called Daglish and was just a general cargo ship. Unescorted, we sailed on the tide to Methil again. It was strange that no ship I was on had ever been attacked on this run. The coast was littered with wrecks; I was just lucky I suppose. We left Methil immediately for Loch Ewe, where the convoy was waiting for us.

The Jarrow men in the crew weren't friends of mine; the only two I knew at all were a fireman called Blackie and another named McGinley. I really missed the Flowergate crowd, even Joe Jordan and his South Shields cronies. I'd somehow formed a bond of trust with them; there's something stimulating about a mutual rivalry. Even an artificial one based on territory. They go on all over the world.

Most of all, I missed Sammy with his trouble-making, laughter, and praying.

I think I was mourning the past. I'd heard while at home that Paddy Connelly, my old mate from the Marconi, had been lost at sea. Nor could I find out where Tommy Devine was--no one had heard of him for a while. The rumour was that he too had gone. A lot of my previous shipmates had perished.

Two days out, we heard we were bound for New York, which was great as far as I was concerned. I decided that when we arrived I would jump ship and get the hell away to the middle of the U.S., somewhere they'd never think of looking for a British sailor. In the meantime we shovelled coal.

Blackie loved to drink; it was all he lived for. Once he was in the 'tween deck,' the half-landing storeroom from which coal is shovelled to the bunkers below. He was loading the black stuff onto a chute down to the stokehole when he noticed a locked iron door. He asked me to go up and pretend to be shovelling, but really to try to see where the door led. I had no idea. It had nuts, bolts and a few screws, but seemed simple enough to open.

'It's probably to the linen room,' I said dismissively.

'I'm going to draw a plan of the ship and work out what it is.' said Blackie. He was taking measurements for days. I paid no attention. We'd had a couple of scares from the siren, and I was trying to catch up with sleep.

Blackie had an air of elation about him when we went on watch. 'Bill, I've worked out where that door leads, it's to the bond.'

Although we civilians were never given the tot of rum that the Navy ratings got, the ship's officers had all the wine and brandy they wanted. Blackie's eyes sparkled at the thought.

'We could go in and take out whatever we wanted to drink, then close the door after us. No one would ever know.'

I was a beer drinker, so it wasn't of much interest to me, but Blackie wanted someone to share this project. Each watch, we took turns in firing the furnaces while the other went up to the tween deck to move coal and work fast at undoing the screws and locks. I began to get interested despite myself. After two days, Blackie managed to get the door open, but only about three inches.

'I can't see what's holding it, maybe you can.'

I lay on the floor and saw a heavy rope tied to the door, but not where it went at the other end. 'You'll need a long knife, Blackie. You'll have to wait until we get ashore. You can open it on the way back.'

'Oh bugger that; the cook's got one with a long handle. I'll borrow it.'

The job was getting too big for the two of us, so we let in the other two members of our watch--Jimmie McGinly and Budgy Woodhouse--who'd been wondering why we were being so furtive. By this time, we were being attacked by subs, and the convoy sirens were sounding every day. One merchant ship was sunk, but all four of us Bond breakers must have been as insane as each other--we ignored everything except the methods of getting at the bonded booze. Tunnel vision they call it now.

Blackie stole the knife, only to discover that it just reached to the rope but wouldn't go far enough to cut it. So someone tied it to a stick and that did the trick. When he started sawing, though, the knot came apart; the knife fell into the other room, where no one could reach it, so Blackie went to steal a big fork from the galley.

He found the cook raising hell about his stolen knife. 'You must have dropped it behind a stove,' was the agreed opinion, but the cook knew he hadn't.

'Maybe the galley has a ghost?' I suggested.

Unfortunately, the fork tines had to be bent into a hook shape to get the knife back, and so the fork couldn't be returned to the galley.

We'd reached Halifax, and to my surprise I hadn't experienced my usual fear. We hadn't opened the door, but Blackie was saving up his dishonourable intentions for the way back. I hoped I'd be in Middle America somewhere.

The cook had a constant watch on the galley by now. 'What shall we do with the knife and fork?' asked Blackie.

'Throw the bastards overboard,' I said. So he did.

We went down the coast to New York. The Chief Steward came down to our mess before we docked in Brooklyn. 'I just want the clever bastards who have been trying to break into the Bond to know we've been onto you for two weeks. We've been waiting for you, and if you'd managed to get in you'd be in handcuffs by now.'

He knew who'd started it. Blackie and I got a bad behaviour report from that ship. It never came back to haunt Blackie though; his luck was running out.

We went on day-cleaning watches; mine was from 10:00 am to 3:00 PM. I did my share with the boilers, and then I went with Blackie and McGinley on the ferry from Brooklyn across to Hoboken, where we found a saloon we liked and stopped for a drink. The proprietor, Tony, was a fat Italian, who we thought was pretty thick. Cheeky that; we weren't in any position to judge anyone's intelligence.

He asked where, what, why, and then happily bought beers for us, while Blackie and McGinley told stories of their trips. It was a small price to pay, especially as McGinley had the gift of blowing trivia into an epic. I couldn't be bothered; I was sick of the bloody war.

At one stage Tony said, 'Oh, boy, do you think you could get me some souvenirs of the war? I'll pay for them.'

We couldn't think immediately of anything, but we promised to come back the next afternoon with something.

After we left, McGinley said, 'We could get into the ammunition store, you know. Those soldiers keep the keys in their cabin.'

That was a great idea we all thought. There isn't a lot on a ship to pinch.

The soldiers were ashore when we got back to the Amberton, so we got the keys and opened the ammunition locker. It was a bit of a disappointment, though, because there wasn't any small manageable souvenir in sight. The shells, which must have been for the Bofors, were about twelve inches long. We debated a bit, but that was all there was to take.

'We'll take two,' I said, 'We don't know if it's the sort of thing he'd like.'

'Any souvenir collector would love them,' Blackie said. 'If we're going to take them, we may as well have enough. Perhaps some of his friends would like to buy one. Let's take six.'

McGinley objected. 'There'll be none left for if we're attacked on the way back.'

'Doesn't matter, these bastards couldn't hit anything anyway.'

We carefully packed them into kit bags to go back to the saloon; they were extremely heavy, so we took turns carrying them. We got onto the ferry but McGinley was fed up.

'There's too many of the bloody things; we'll have to dump a couple.'

'Where? Someone will see us.'

'Let's go to the stern. If we all lean over the rail, they won't know what we're doing.'

I looked over and saw the propeller churning away. Blackie said, 'If we drop it here and it hits the propellers, it'll blow the bloody stern off the ship.'

'And us with it. We'd better think again', I said. The ferry started to pull in so we took them ashore and eventually wrapped and then left them in a container marked TRASHCAN.

'That's better,' said McGinley. 'Good thing you thought of that propeller, Blackie.'

The bar had a lot of customers. 'We've got you a couple of souvenirs,' McGinley told Tony.

His big fat face lit up. 'Oh swell. Come into the back room.'

He opened the sack and pulled out a shell. His eyes nearly popped out and then his expression turned to fear. 'Jesus Christ,' he stuttered, 'These are live shells.'

'They're good souvenirs,' said Blackie indignantly.

'If I'm caught with these, I'll get ninety-nine years in Leavenworth.' He put the shell back in the bag, trying to hustle us to the door at the same time. 'Get out, get out! I don't know you and don't come back here.' Fear had caused rivulets of sweat to run down his face.

We were out in the street again. 'That didn't go down too well,' I said. 'What'll we do now?'

'I need a drink,' said Blackie. 'We'll think about it then.'

So we hauled the shells to another bar, had a couple of beers, and got quite mellow. Then we went on to another bar, had a couple more, and left for another joint.

'Who has the shells?' I asked at one point.

'I thought you did,' said McGinley.

'Christ, I left them at that last bar,' said Blackie. We hurried back to find the kit bag still sitting safely under the table. It was then we sat down and decided that the shells must go back to the ship-- perhaps two might not be missed, but six most certainly would. Having decided their fate, we all promptly forgot about them.

We woke up next day on the ship.

Where had we left the shells? God alone knows. We hadn't heard any explosions. We worked from 10:00 am to 3:00 PM and then we went on deck. As usual, the soldiers were polishing their gun.

They were in and out of the shell locker, but no one said anything. The keys were no longer in sight. I realised that if they reported the loss, they'd be in trouble for carelessness in leaving the keys available to light fingers. I had the theory that they would pray for a plane attack on the ship so they'd have a chance to fire the guns and cover themselves.

Blackie muttered, 'They'll never need the shells. They're not going to dirty that bloody gun.'

After a couple of trouble free days, McGinley said, 'Come to think of it, it's disgraceful those soldiers losing ammunition like that and not reporting it.'

The whole incident sends shudders up my spine even now.

Four days later, I went alone to Union City, where I got legless drunk. I came out of the last bar looking for a place to sleep it off, and slumped into a dark doorway with my back against the door. I must have triggered the burglar alarm, because within three minutes a police car containing two extra large cops stopped.

'Where are you from, buddy?'

'Hoboken,' I croaked. I didn't think to mention the ship, which turned out to be fortunate.

'He's not breaking in; he's just drunk. Let's put him in the tank.'

They dragged me to the precinct, and put me into one of the eight cages along a corridor. I slept like a baby until the morning; I didn't even dream.

When I woke, one prisoner was saying, 'It's the third time that bitch has had me in this month. I'm going to kill her!'

'Why did she call the police?' another asked.

'I just gave her a bit of a slap.' He was being charged with wife beating, someone else with armed robbery. The rest of us were drunk--in my case drunk and incapable. They gave us coffee and a bun, and then we went before a judge.

It was a Sunday court, especially designed for Saturday night drunks. The atmosphere was most informal.

'What's the charge?' asked the judge.

'Drunk and incapable. We answered an alarm and found him slumped in the doorway going to sleep. He was in no condition to break in anywhere.'

'I'm going to fine you five dollars, Linskey. I'm tired of you Polacks from Hoboken coming here every Saturday night to raise hell. If you come before me again, I'll put you in the workhouse for thirty days. Just keep the hell out of Union City in future.'

Although the prospect of a workhouse was appealing enough, this wouldn't go on my ship record, thank God. He had a nerve though, I thought, calling an Irishman a Polack.

I decided that I'd jump ship and join up with Pat Shaughnessy in Manhattan. When I arrived, his grandmother welcomed me but told me he wasn't there. 'He went out one day and we haven't heard a word since. He'll turn up sometime, I expect.'

Typical Irish. They've historically been used to family disappearing off the face of the earth. The lost ones usually rolled back several months or years later.

Manhattan wasn't the same without my mates, and as I was short of money by now I sadly made my way back to the Amberton. I would have to desert next time.

The next day we left for Halifax. We were two days at sea when Blackie suddenly jerked upright in his bunk. 'I just remembered my name's printed on that kit-bag the shells were in. They'll throw the book at me.'

'Never,' I said. 'Black's a very common name--there must be millions of them in the service.'

'Not with their address at 15 Salem Street, Jarrow, England,' he said glumly.

He never found out if he'd been discovered, though. He was lost at sea on his next trip.

The cook had it in for us now. The Chief Steward had told him about the knives. 'You and Blackie stole my knives and you didn't have the decency to replace them,' he scolded us.

He made some mention of it at every meal and appeared intent on picking a fight with me, although he weighed about twenty pounds less than I did and it didn't seem likely he would. The fourth repetition was too much for me, however, and I said, 'Oh shut up, you spotty faced git. You're enough to turn anyone off their food.'

'Right, out on deck.' Everyone followed happily, all thought of food forgotten.

'Christ, he's contemplating suicide,' I thought--what a patronising bastard I was. 'I'll go a bit easy on him; he's too light for me.'

Someone shouted, 'Make a circle. Take your shoes off, no kicking.'

I noticed we had an audience on the bridge, but no attempt was made to stop us.

Cook took a sparring stance, his hands covering his face. I went to hit him thinking, 'I'll finish this quickly and put him out of his misery.'

But it didn't work out quite like that. My first punch missed him altogether; he just moved his head, and I couldn't understand how I'd failed to hit him. I closed in, thinking I'd carry his head off with this one, but his arms forestalled the punch before it travelled very far. Quick as a flash, he hit me on the side of the face. I hadn't seen it coming. It didn't hurt, but it ruffled my dignity. I'd have to take this more seriously.

I went towards him, and he danced away. I was mentally pleading with him to stand still, so I could catch him. It felt as though he had ten arms. I threw another right and a left, but his arms blocked both of them. Then he gave me another punch under my bottom lip, which drew blood. I hadn't even landed one on him yet.

This went on for about six minutes. He ducked and dived and landed the odd punch, which had no chance of knocking me out, but was humiliating. Every time he avoided my fists and gave me a little smack in return, there was a cheer from the onlookers. I was definitely the bad guy in this fight.

By this time, I was getting tired and worried. 'God, if I'm beaten by someone twenty pounds lighter, I'll never lift my head again.' As I kept hitting his arms, I felt like a bloody clown. I was beginning to learn a few of his moves, though, and I managed to anticipate one or two blows. So I tried a new tactic. I pretended to throw one at his face, stopped midway, as his hands went up to protect himself and threw a wonderful punch to his ribs. I heard the air whoosh out of his lungs. As his hands came down I followed up with what I intended to be a blow under his chin, which was exposed. Even then, he had enough savvy to move his head and my fist landed on his cheekbone. He went down, but he was conscious. He made a half-hearted attempt to get up, but slumped back.

'Jesus, I can't. I'm fucked.'

I gave him a hand up. 'Thank Christ for that. So am I.'

We went to the galley to wash. 'I'm sorry I called you a spotty faced git,' I told him.

'That's all right. It was a good fight, though, wasn't it?'

It certainly was. Next day one of the deckhands said, 'We could have told you he knew how to fight. The Scousers all stay clear of him. He was a welterweight boxer in the Army before the war.'

I felt a bit better then; at least I knew why he was so hard to hit.

I was right too about him wanting to pick a fight. Blackie told me most of the crew had been waiting for it. The Liverpool mob had money on the cook to win, but the Shields and Sunderland lot trusted to my reputation and backed me. They'd never know how close it had been. I did tell the cook, though, and we became quite friendly after that. He said he'd expected to tire me out, which was what usually happened with untrained fighters. He'd begun to despair as I kept on coming. I assured him that I was despairing at the same time.

'How do you feel?' I asked.

'I think my ribs are up near my shoulder blades, but apart from that I'm okay.'

'If I'd lost that fight, I'd have had to throw myself overboard,' I said.

'Yes, you *are* an arrogant bastard. I heard the skipper was very disappointed too that you didn't lose.'

I'd learned a lesson--never to judge a man's courage or fighting ability by his appearance. I promised myself that I'd learn to box, but I never did. I remained a street brawler.

We had other things to worry about over the next week. A ship was being picked off every couple of days by a sub. We didn't know how many there were, and it was a constant worry.

However, the *Amberton* survived, and we went on to dock at Newport in South Wales. I went up to Jarrow by train to stay with my father, who'd moved further up the same street. He was now working at the dry dock for Palmer's Shipbuilding and getting well paid, which meant my new suit hadn't been pawned. Yet.

When I'd seen Pat's grandmother in Manhattan, she said she had forwarded a Canadian letter to England for me. A shame that was, she said--if she'd known I was coming she'd have kept it. This letter had now arrived and Da was really pleased. It was from my brother, Austin. Da always thought Austin had deserted him, even though he himself had encouraged the young man to go to Canada.

Austin said he'd been overwhelmed to hear from us after all these years. Had he known I was in New York, he'd have come down to see me. He was working in a logging camp. He'd tried to join the army, but had been refused because of his varicose veins. He didn't say if he was married.

Da and I went for a drink to celebrate, and we ran into Marty Shaughnessy, Pat's father, who told us Pat had worked his way home on a Swedish ship. I went round to see him the next day. It turned out he'd been on Ellis Island when I was in New York. He'd been picked up as an illegal immigrant and was in the process of being deported. He couldn't let his Gran know, because the Immigration kept asking him where he'd been living. He couldn't tell because the family would have been charged with harbouring an illegal. They asked him if he wanted to work his way home on the Swedish ship rather than be deported, and of course he accepted. If he'd been deported, he'd never get back into the U.S.

Chapter 12

PQ18 Convoy.
SS Empire Beaumont.

I didn't bother to report to the Pool while I had some money. When it ran out, I went to the shipping officer and got the usual abuse for not coming earlier. He said there were two ships at Newcastle and they would be signing on crew, so I went to the shipping office.

'I do have something that might appeal more to you, though,' the shipping master said. 'But it's strictly for volunteers.'

Volunteers! No way would I volunteer for anything ever. Jesus, what deadly cargo was it carrying that they wanted volunteers? Nevertheless, I asked what it was.

'It's a bit hard to explain. This ship is in Archangel, Russia, and never goes to sea. It carries an eighty-ton heavy lifting Jumbo crane and moves from quay to quay unloading planes and tanks from Allied ships.'

I was suspicious. 'You mean this crane ship will be in one river, one port?'

'Yes. It's right up your alley if you're fed up with trips. It should be unsinkable, but if the worst happened you could swim to shore. You have to sign a two-year contract, though.'

I thought about it and it appealed to me. At that time, Russia was the home of hope to many people. Germany was the evil fascist, but the Soviet Union was the new Utopia. Communism represented progress. Working people would get a fair deal and a proper education. Best of all, I'd be in harbour within sight of land all the time. The more firma the less terror. It seemed a bloody sight better proposition than sailing through the U-boat packs.

'It sounds all right,' I said.

'You don't have to go,' he repeated. 'It's for two years and it isn't entirely safe. There'll be air raids because the Germans will be trying to knock out the docks.'

'I don't mind if I'm on land.'

'Articles are being signed tomorrow.'

I felt elated on the way back to Jarrow. This would really be a different adventure. I met Pat at Kelley's Bar and told him all about it.

'I wouldn't mind doing that,' he said. 'I wonder if there's another job?'

'I don't think he has a full crew. You might as well come with me.'

The next morning, we went to sign on. In the shipping office, a sign had been on the walls ever since Russia became an ally: 'Any seaman who can speak Russian will be paid bonus money.'

'Some chance,' said Pat, 'Have you ever heard it spoken? Even their alphabet's different.' The shipping officer assured him they had a place and were suspiciously eager to get another volunteer. We signed on and were given an advance note. They advised us to bring very warm clothing, because the winters were severe in the Arctic Circle. We were going up as passengers not as crew. That was something to look forward to.

Instead of buying warm clothes, however, we cashed in our notes and drank the money, so my kit consisted of a spare pair of dungarees, two vests, underwear, and a couple of sweat rags. Pat's was just as meagre. Neither of us had a suitcase, so we carried both lots in a brown paper carrier bag. We had to muster at Newcastle Railway station, where we would catch a train to our embarkation.

We dropped into Kelley's for a last drink, where my Aunt Mima, a pretty forty-year old woman who'd been widowed for about three years, was drinking with some friends.

'We're on our way to Russia,' I told her.

'Is that your luggage?' she said pointing to the carrier bag.

'Yes. Why?'

'It's not going to keep you very warm. You're both crazy.'

Her son John Nee, my cousin, came in looking for her. John was just sixteen and dying to grow up and see the world.

'If I had the fare, I'd come up to Newcastle to see you off,' he said. I still had some money, so I said I'd pay his fare.

He was happy as hell, telling us on the way that he wanted to go to sea. He was a tall boy who looked a bit older than his age.

Thirty of us mustered in Newcastle, where we heard that an ordinary seaman hadn't turned up.

'Do you think I could go?' John asked me.

'Don't be crazy,' I said, 'We could run into trouble. And you're too young.'

'You went to sea when you were seventeen.'

'There wasn't a war on. And you're only sixteen.'

He persisted, ' So are cabin boys. And mess-room boys. Oh, go on. Please, Bill. Ask him can I go.'

I said to the First Mate, 'How about this lad? He's never been to sea, but he badly wants to come. He's my cousin.'

The Mate asked his age.

'I'm seventeen, almost eighteen,' said John. Just a year and a big bit off the truth.

The Mate looked dubious but didn't want to go one short in his crew. 'Okay,' he agreed.

John was really pleased, but I doubted that Mima would be. We went to Glasgow by train and then to Greenock by bus, driving right in through the dock gates into a big disembarkation shed. We weren't allowed to leave there. In the afternoon, we were given refreshments. We passed the time gambling, and I won thirteen pounds. Pat also had a win of eight pounds. We both sent it to our fathers as it wasn't going to be any use to us for two years, but we found out much later Pat's father Marty never received his.

The crew for the crane ship in Russia was split into two. John went to the SS Ocean Faith, while Pat and I boarded the SS Empire Beaumont. I wanted John to sail with us, but it wasn't possible. He was so young, I would have been happier if he had been under my protection. I think he may have been the youngest boy to have signed up for 'Active Service' which is what the Russian contract was.

The holds were filled with cargo - I don't know what it was - and every inch of deck space was covered with tanks and small planes. Quarters for we passengers had been built midship on the tween deck just below water level, where we were very comfortable. Pat was the only one of the fifteen men I knew, but we soon became friendly with a cook called Sheriff and a seaman called Tosh. There were two Shields men, one of whom kept us entertained with his prodigious memory--he could recite poems such as 'Dan McGrew,' as well as the whole of the dirty rhyme 'Eskimo Nell.' He entertained us for hours; it was like having a holiday and the food was good too.

The six ships sailed in convoy to Loch Ewe, where we picked up a few more. We left on 2nd September 1942 and headed to Reykjavik in Iceland. There we waited--without leave--for the

American Liberty ships that were joining the convoy. The Americans were now sending enormous amounts of armaments to Russia, not that they always got through. There were so many ships in Reykjavik that it looked as though you could travel for miles by jumping from one deck to another. There were many more escort ships than Merchantmen. Our convoy was called the PQ18 and had forty cargo ships, but there were also brand-new American fast destroyers, battleships, and cruisers, as well as The Avenger, an Aircraft Carrier, and an anti-aircraft naval vessel called The Scylla. The scuttlebutt was that there were three escorts for every merchant ship. It was a massive fleet. You would think it impossible for a sub to penetrate a ring of steel like this.

'Doesn't it give you a feeling of confidence?' Pat asked, indicating the Armada.

The pessimist in me replied, 'I'd be more confident if they felt we didn't need them.'

The Allies had lost five million tons of shipping so far in 1942, and in June alone a ship was going down every four hours. Worse still, the Germans announced that soon there would be four hundred new U-boats in service.

No doubt I'd have had more confidence if I hadn't heard about the previous convoy to Russia, the PQ17, which had been a disaster. Thirty-nine Merchant ships escorted by minesweepers, trawlers, destroyers, anti-aircraft, corvettes, and two submarines had left on 27th June. The convoy was detected and the sub attack started on 1st July, escalating until three merchant ships were lost on 4th July. This attack was repelled with what was considered slight loss by the Admiralty, if not by the families of the dead seamen. However, the convoy was still in good spirits and good order until an Admiralty order came to scatter. The command came as a terrible shock to the Escort. Worse, it was based on faulty intelligence as to the movements of the enemy surface forces. After the order was obeyed, the Germans were able to roam at will around the convoy, sinking the near defenceless merchant ships. Twenty-one went down between 5th and 10th July, making a total of twenty-four. The reports didn't bother to say how many seamen had died. They never did.

As the dreadful story trickled through, our confidence in the infallibility of our Armada faded. It'd be okay perhaps, as long as they stayed with us and no stupid bastard at the Admiralty ordered them off on a false alarm. With all these ships, we felt as though we were going into a major battle. As merchant seamen, we'd been unable to fight back and now, as a civilian passenger, I felt even worse. We were just helpless prey; I couldn't even shovel coal at breakneck speed to get the bloody ship across the water. There were four more passengers, two Czech Air force officers and two women. They had an air of confidence about them--they must have been Embassy officials or something similar.

One seaman said, 'That's a bad omen. Women on a ship always bring bad luck.'

I replied, 'Thanks a lot. I've had enough bad luck already.'

'Couldn't have been all that bad--you've survived.'

We were in Reykjavik a few days, until we shipped out on 8th September. The ships kept fairly close together, and we were near enough The Empire Stevenson to yell to the crew, which included a lot of Geordies. Many of us knew each other, and I made arrangements to meet a couple of friends at the nearest pub when we docked.

As we discovered later, the convoy had been located on 8th September by a German reconnaissance plane from Norway. Our first indication was on the 10th, when we saw a plane flying in circles around the convoy, well out of the range of guns. The pilot had plenty of time to radio back to his control, giving the position, the number of armed ships, and the make-up of the Merchant convoy. After thirty minutes that felt like hours, he disappeared, no doubt returning to the Norwegian base for refuelling.

It was beautiful September weather—calm seas and blue skies, with just enough fluffy white clouds to look great—and it remained so for a couple of days. We knew we were being stalked, but we proceeded rapidly in proper formation.

On September 12th, we heard that the destroyers had sunk a submarine ahead of the convoy. Then at midday on the 13th, the siren screamed ACTION STATIONS! Pat and I were drinking a cup of tea in our mess. Although passengers, we had of course each been given an Action Station—we were to be on deck, passing ammunition up to the naval gunners manning the stern gun. The ammunition was sent up by pulley, and we stood on top of the armoury with the open door giving us a full view of the various weapons of destruction. I tried to keep my mind off the possibility of a direct hit on all that ammo.

Pat grumbled, 'I wish they'd close that bloody door.'

Suddenly hell broke loose. Bombs were raining down on us from nowhere, but we couldn't see the planes. They didn't hit anything as far as I know, and were so far out of sight that there was no accuracy at all. Their purpose was purely to demoralise, and it succeeded all too well with me. Then the dive-bombers screamed down and the terrible crack of the explosives hit like a punch to the head and body.

When they'd unloaded their bombs and gone away, presumably to refuel, there came a most awesome sight—an approaching black cloud of torpedo bombing planes. Forty-four of them flew in low, barely skimming the water as they fired on us, with cannon, guns and torpedoes.

Oh Jesus, God Almighty. We ran into the mess room. When we looked out, we could see goggled faces, so close they must have been only forty feet away. Salvos of shells were strafing the mess room. Glass shattered, bullets ricocheted, wooden furniture splintered.

For the first time in action, I felt my own mortality. I thought the planes were aiming straight at me personally. I saw distinctly the face of one of the German pilots. I was deaf and terrified.

That wave passed, and in the lull we had one thought—we were too close to the armoury. The terrific smell of cordite was choking me. It smelled as though all things on earth were burning up. We ran along the deck looking for more shelter. The wave of torpedo planes came by again. I didn't see the drop of the one that hit us.

Pat was about seven feet behind me when there was a terrific bang and a flash of light. I looked back and to my horror saw Pat and Sheriff blown over the side. I was sick with fear and misery. I was sure Pat was dead, but I could do nothing except run towards my allocated lifeboat.

It was on fire, so when I saw another one being lowered I climbed into that. The eight of us in the boat rowed like demented creatures to get away before the ship exploded. The torpedo had hit The Beaumont, leaving a massive hole exactly where we'd been drinking tea fifteen minutes earlier. Now she was burning from stem to stern. Absurdly, I felt glad I hadn't bought warm clothes, but then I started worrying about Pat. I'd completely forgotten my young cousin, John Nee.

Some German subs had taken advantage of the din to penetrate the defences and were now among the merchant ships. Suddenly I saw The Empire Stevenson, with the Tyneside crew, explode and quickly sink. It must have been carrying ammunition. All hands were lost. I was already shell-shocked, and the ear shattering noise was driving me crazy. I nursed my head in my hands, trying to block out some of the din. The battle was still raging. German bombs and shells, as well as the guns on every one of our seventy-five or so escort vessels were firing. In the lifeboat of the Ashby, I'd felt reasonably safe, but now there was such a lot of crossfire from ships trying to hit the new wave of low flying torpedo planes. In the panic, they often hit each other and God knows how many own goals were scored.

The second wave of torpedo planes came out. Ships were sinking and burning and the sea was full of shouting and screaming men. The noise was unceasing, as though the loudest explosion in the world was continuing unbroken for twenty minutes. A sub surfaced and an American merchant ship started firing at it. They missed, but strafed right along the side of another merchantman. I saw a German torpedo plane floating on the water with three men standing on the wings waving for rescue. A naval vessel speeded towards it and both plane and men disappeared.

Eventually, the enemy returned to base and we were able to take stock. We'd saved more men from the water and now we numbered twenty in the boat. Rescue ships were picking up other survivors. The sea was filled with lifeboats, rafts, hatch covers, life belts, oil, debris of all descriptions.

And bodies. Everywhere there were bodies.

PART THREE:
THE FROZEN NORTH
ARCHANGEL, RUSSIA 1942-1943

Chapter 13
SS Empire Bard.

Only the dead were silent—the wounded were screaming to be rescued. But there was one piece of luck. Even though the sea was still bloody cold, there was some summer warmth left in it; three months later, anyone overboard would have died within minutes.

A destroyer with nets over the side finally picked us up. Then it raced back to the convoy and transferred us to the fleet-sweeper *Sharpshooter*. This was a purpose-built minesweeper, unlike the many trawlers that had been converted. Once aboard, we were sent below to sit between the sailors' bunks, where we stayed for four days, along with other Russian, American, and Polish survivors. There were too many of us to lie down, and those able to sleep did so sitting up. We were allowed up on deck only occasionally for a breath of air.

I was in shock and unable to think clearly. I felt like a man about to be executed, praying for a reprieve. There must have been thirty men in this small space, but there was silence. I didn't hear a word spoken. There was no food, and no one wanted any. Just let us live. We knew that with the dark that the planes wouldn't be attacking, so I prayed for nightfall. Unfortunately, there aren't many hours of darkness in summer as you head north.

In the past, I'd felt more of an observer of the war, but now I hated the Germans. I wanted them all to be killed in any possible way. I didn't care that they too might be young and frightened. No one in the world could have been more frightened than I was. If by any chance I survived this attack and got back to the UK, nothing would get me aboard another ship. They could jail me for life.

The sirens went again early on the 14th September when the Oiler *Atheltemplar* was hit by a torpedo. Later, another torpedo attack was frustrated and scuttlebutt said that twelve aircraft were brought down. Another colossal explosion was the sinking of the *Mary Luckenback*. She must have been carrying ammunition and she disintegrated. The blast came down the stairway of our ship, and everything hanging, such as curtains and hammocks, straightened out to horizontal. The breath whooshed out of our lungs. All the oxygen was vacuumed out of the air, and for a few seconds we couldn't breathe.

Two Naval ratings came down, visibly shocked. 'Christ, wasn't that terrible?'

We asked what had happened. One of them shook his head and said, 'You don't really want to know. It's too horrible.'

I had never considered joining any service where one swore to obey orders without question. I suppose that deep down I knew I was incapable of such discipline and had not the ability to say 'Yes sir, no sir.' But during the next few days when the attacks continued I learned to admire these Royal Navy ratings. They remained calm, efficient, and extremely brave. I was very impressed. Some of them were continuously doing these Russian convoys, and the war must have seemed endless to them.

Again we heard sirens on the 15th September and more dive-bombers. There was a loud explosion and I thought we'd been torpedoed. Then it went quiet again. A rating came down and told us that a dive-bomber had just missed us. We only heard it; we saw nothing. It was never quiet--always the sound of depth charges, guns firing, planes being hit, and subs blowing up. Nothing like that first massive attack, though.

The ratings never had more than an hour's rest and not much time for food. We got the odd cup of tea and biscuit and once a ham sandwich. It didn't matter that much--no one was hungry. Even sleeping was impossible; if I dropped into a sitting doze, it was always straight into a nightmare. Awake though, a great calm had descended on me; I was almost catatonic. I couldn't even hear people speaking, maybe because I spent most of the remainder of the trip with my fingers in my ears.

As we got closer to Russia, some ships broke from the convoy to go to Murmansk, leaving the rest to continue to Archangel. I transferred with the rest of the crew of *The Empire Bard* to the *Daneman*, a converted trawler that was really rotten. There were fourteen of us, which made it grossly overcrowded too. We were harassed all the way up through the White Sea, but the planes finally departed at the mouth of the River Dvina.

We weren't allowed ashore for four days until our identities were checked, and the wounded saw Russian doctors. Those of us with what were considered light wounds—meaning we could walk and eat—had no medical attention. We'd docked in a small logging town, but all we could see from the decks were ramshackle wooden houses and timber yards stretching for miles. Nevertheless, I felt safe here. I heard that John's ship had arrived safely, which relieved me of one burden of guilt; I could have never faced Mima if he'd been lost. I was very upset about Pat, though—I was sure he'd been killed.

After four days, they took us to Archangel in a dreadful old van with torn seats. The roads were only dirt tracks, and how this vehicle held together on all the bumps I don't know. Sometimes great planks of wood were stretched lengthways to form a firmer surface. We passed one village called Salumbla about three miles out of Archangel, which I would get to know very well in the future. As we got closer to the city, there were some four and five floor buildings and the roads became more solid, with a stone base. Only the main roads of course--the side roads were still just packed dirt.

A priest from the Mission to Seamen met us at the *Intourist* Hotel. After we registered, he took us to a big store run by the Mission within the hotel, and we chose some clothes. I took a fur-lined leather airman's jacket. I couldn't wear it then because it was still too warm, but I knew I was going to need it later. We got shirts, underwear, and everything else we needed. I believe the clothes had been collected by the Women's Voluntary Services (WVS), who with The Mission to Seamen did a wonderful job during the war.

Food had been prepared for us. The first course was fish soup. Yuk! I'd never heard of it in my life and it tasted bloody horrible, so I left it. I wouldn't have believed how short a time it would be before I was glad to eat it. Then we had a kind of omelette that was full of potatoes. Tea from a samovar served in a glass was the next novelty; it was really sweet with no milk, and I drank glass after glass. Finally we had *blinis*, little pancakes that were also extremely sweet.

I felt great, apart from my stinking body and clothes. We hadn't washed for weeks and fear has its own smell. I shared a room with three others, and we all dumped the clothes that hadn't been off our backs for the last fortnight. The baths, showers and lavatories were in one block on our floor; there was plenty of hot water and we'd each been given a bar of carbolic soap. I soaked in that bath until the water turned cold; it was wonderful. Then I dressed in clean clothes; I had been issued with an identity pass, and all I needed now was a walk to stretch my legs.

The population of Archangel at this time was around 100,000. The streets were full, but there were only women and old men. Some were obviously pitifully poor, but even the women who were reasonably clad wore clothes from a date long before I started noticing female attire. A little row of shops opposite *Intourist* had a dressmaker; a watchmaker, a barber, a sewing machine repairer, and a cobbler— private enterprise wasn't totally dead in the USSR then. The bigger shops had no food or clothes, however, and the only full shelves contained some old books that didn't look very inviting. They were either political tracts or propaganda about the amount of wheat grown somewhere, and it didn't help that they were in the Cyrillic alphabet.

Then I looked up and saw Pat approaching. I couldn't believe my eyes.

We just stood grinning at each other for a few minutes, shaking hands. I was choked with emotion. I couldn't speak and nor could he.

'Christ am I glad to see you!' I eventually managed to splutter. 'I thought you were dead when I saw you go over the side.'

'Me too,' he said. ' I mean that I thought *you* were. Hell, let's get a drink! I know where we can buy some vodka.'

As we walked along, we passed three young giggling girls Pat knew. I couldn't believe my ears when he spoke to them in RUSSIAN! My mouth must have dropped open and the girls giggled and one spoke to me. '*Kak vasha eemya,*' it sounded like.

'She's saying, 'What's your name?'' Pat was tickled pink to be able to translate, and I was eaten up with jealousy. They were the first Russian words I'd ever heard.

'Bill,' I replied to her question, and the girls burst into giggles. 'Beel, Beel,' more giggles. I could see that Bill meant something funny in Russian, but it was some days before I discovered it just was the Russian word for 'was.' Not that much of a joke.

Pat bought a bottle of vodka, and we went to a park to drink it and hear each other's misadventures.

'I was dazed when I hit the water,' he told me, 'From the blast, I suppose. When I looked around, I saw a raft with three men so I swam to it. There was a big swell, but they helped me aboard. I was just relieved to be on it—there were bodies all around me in the water. I spied Sheriff waving about fifty yards away and I shouted, 'Swim over here!' but he probably didn't hear with all the clamour, because he was yelling, 'Use your paddles!'

'The other men told me that the paddles must have gone overboard. We couldn't move the heavy raft with our hands, so we all shouted, "Come towards us!" Then Sheriff called again, "Use your paddles!" "We have no paddles!" we replied. This went on for some minutes, and then Sheriff had gone. A rescue ship picked me up. I've been here about a week.'

Pat was very emotional when recounting this story; it's awful to see anyone die in front of your eyes and be unable to help. I choked up too; I'd liked Sheriff, who was to have been the cook on the *Empire Bard*. I found myself almost envying women their ability to wrap their arms about a friend and cry some of the pain away with them. We drank vodka instead.

'There's one good thing; the bastards can't stop our pay for being sunk,' said Pat.

'Why not?'

'Because we weren't signed on. We weren't crew.'

That gave me great pleasure.

John, my cousin, was really glad to see me. He had seen the Empire Beaumont burning from stem to stern and was sure that Pat and I had perished.

John said, 'I felt like an abandoned child, scared to death in this hostile world that suddenly I had been plunged into.'

Actually during the month since I last saw him he seemed to have matured way beyond his years. He had become his own man; he'd chummed up with some others of the Empire Bard crew and hung about with them. It suited us, because he didn't drink much and drink was our prime objective.

He served out his contract with the Empire Bard in a responsible manner.

Pat and I were rounded up with the rest of the *Empire Bard* replacement crew that evening and told that we'd stay on in the *Intourist* hotel for about a week. There was an International Club across the street with dancing, billiards, a restaurant, and concerts. We could even buy vodka, usually not very much because of rationing. When anything ran out, you got no more of it until stocks were replenished anything from days to weeks later.

The first night, we went to the International Club, where a quartet was playing—two old men and two old women. One woman played the balalaika, the other a violin. The pianist was a thin frail old man, but the drummer was as solid as a tree, with a neck that looked the size of the pianist's chest. He wore a Russian shirt with buttoning up to the shoulder; I always longed for a shirt like this but never managed to get one. I'd know that pianist now after all these years if I saw him again; his bald head was like a skull.

It was the first live music I'd heard in my life apart from Salvation Army bands and the blues man in Philadelphia. They played Strauss waltzes, Tschaikovsky, and songs from pre-war operettas. I didn't know this music at the time—I only remember my mind and spirit soaring. I don't know how good the quartet was, but I thought I had reached heaven. Perhaps the vodka helped. That was my introduction to Russia, the start of a long love story for me.

The main streets were crowded with foreigners. Archangel was an absolute hodgepodge of seamen from every country. There were Lithuanians, Estonians, and Latvians who had been living and working in other countries before the war. If their ships were sunk and they arrived at Russian ports in Allied ships, the Soviet authorities claimed them as Soviet citizens. They refused to accept this ruling and went on strike. Possibly they weren't arrested because the Allied countries on whose ships they had arrived kept a diplomatic eye on them. They were given a talon every day that entitled them to food, which they ate at the International club. We became friendly with some of them, and they taught us a lot of Russian words.

The Russian civilians had almost nothing to eat. Even with money, there was no food to buy in the shops and the plight of the poor was dreadful. Every time we came out of a restaurant, there were really old people and little children asking for food. After my first meal, I learned to wrap up any bread left on the table and take it with me for the eager hands waiting outside. There were also old men and women in the streets with great folded wads of roubles wanting to buy anything. Money didn't seem very hard to get, but goods were impossible. I had to sell a shirt I'd got from the Seamen's Mission so as to have spending money. As well as these old people, there were black marketers—what the British called 'spivs' and the Russians 'speculators.' They had a small exchange place down near the riverside, where they kept a sharp lookout for the police, who would jail them. In Russia, speculators were really serious criminals, as they were engaged in profiteering.

I turned in early that first night in Archangel. The bed was comfortable, and I had the first proper sleep for three weeks; I'd even drunk enough vodka to blot out the nightmares. Perhaps this medicinal effect was unfortunate, because I certainly began to take advantage of that excuse now.

On the second night, German planes carrying incendiary bombs made a massive attack. We were drinking in the *Intourist* when the raid started, and we went outside to see what was happening. This wooden town really would go flash puff, particularly the wooden docks where the big convoy was still unloading. As in ports all over the world, this district was occupied by the poorest in the community. We helped an old woman pull her pathetic bits out of her burning house. Then Pat, the animal lover, heard a dog barking. There was another old woman crying and pointing, so he dashed in and brought her dog out. She was crying in gratitude. We cleared out houses and helped people for at least a couple of hours. By then the houses had either burnt to the ground or else they were safe.

A Russian official approached us, asked our names, and thanked us. Then we went back for a drink.

I was brooding. 'I can't understand it. I wasn't at all afraid there, yet I can't stand action on board a ship.'

'That's because we had plenty to do,' said Pat. 'We're sitting ducks on board.'

That must have been true. Even on a ship, it never was as bad when I was stoking—I was always too busy trying to keep steam up so we'd get the trip over as fast as possible.

The smell of burning wood lingered for weeks, but that was the last big raid on Archangel for some time, apart from lighter, sporadic episodes. The next serious attack would be when the next convoy unloaded. Murmansk however, down to the south, took a terrible pounding almost every night. It wasn't so far for the planes to go, and they could carry heavier ammunition than incendiaries.

The Empire Bard lay in Bakareesta on the other side of the River Dvina. The next day, we crossed by ferry to start unloading. The American ship to be unloaded berthed at the dock with *The Empire Bard* next to it on the waterside, which discharged the cargo across the ship onto the dock. First the Jumbo crane cleared the jeeps, planes, and tanks from the deck; then the hatch covers were removed and the cargo carefully deposited on the dock. Exceptionally carefully if it was ammunition. This would take a couple of days; then the crane would move to the next dock and the next ship. All we had to do was make enough steam to keep the crane working.

When we came off watch that night we stayed aboard. Apparently there was no danger of bombers, and so the discharging went on all night with lights showing. Raids did come, but only about every five days and usually in daylight, because it was such a long way from Finland. Perhaps they'd given their best with the recent incendiary attack.

The food was good on the *Bard*. Three Chinese who'd been in Archangel for some time replaced Sheriff; they must have come at a bargain price. They'd come to Russia with twenty others on an Empire ship *SS Starlight*, which had been damaged by aircraft at sea and finished off in dock during a raid at Murmansk. All twenty of these Chinese were tiny little men but they were as stubborn as mules. They flatly refused to go back to sea; they wanted to be returned to China overland. Now they'd been in Archangel six months. To hell with life on the ocean wave for them.

Thank God for such mercies; they cooked like angels! What a breeze of a job this was after being on a seagoing ship! All the more reason to wonder about the self-destructive pattern that would emerge; I can only think we were mad as bloody hatters.

After breakfast, we took a blanket and sold it. We could buy stuff on credit from the ship's shop, but all our pay was to be given to us when we signed off in England. As our contracts were for two years, we couldn't wait that long. Of course, we could have had a sub and changed it into roubles, but who would be stupid enough to exchange good sterling when we could get 100 roubles for a box of matches?

Our intention was to buy a bottle of vodka, and return to the ship to do our watch at four. We had to ask about before we found anyone who knew where it could be bought. Eventually, we met two British Army gunners who told us of a small club they believed was only for Russians. Worth a try, they thought. We found the place, which had a wooden floor, a few tables, and the smell of something revolting cooking. The few customers were Russian seamen, who muttered a greeting. They were quite friendly.

A waitress came over, a nice looking young woman. I gave my nicest smile. 'Two vodkas, please.'

She looked at me fixedly and enunciated clearly, 'You are the son of the pious parson.'

I thought I'd have more chance of a drink if I agreed. 'Yes, pet. Can I have two vodkas, please?'

'You are the son of the pious parson,' she repeated. I nodded; Pat's mouth was wide open.

'This pronunciation is good? Yes?'

'Excellent,' I assured her.

She looked puzzled. 'Eggs? Is no good?'

'Oh yes, is very good.' She smiled happily, and went to get us our drinks. Another young waitress came over and somehow we managed—lubricated by a lot of vodka—to find out that the first girl was learning English from books. She'd never before heard it spoken, and the pious parson was the extent of her vocabulary. We left clutching a bottle of vodka with a promise to drop in again when we could.

We arrived back at the ship one hour late for our watch. Other crew were doing our work, but they had to be paid overtime. When the watch finished, we were still drunk. The captain called us up and told us off, but he didn't fine us.

Next day, we managed to get up for our early morning watch, although we had the most God-awful hangovers. 'Should we stroll to the Pious Parson?' Pat said when it was over.

We had a few drinks there, and then we returned to the ship for our night watch. After that, we went to our bunks and passed out. Right out. They couldn't wake us to do our 4:00 am watch, until eventually the engineer succeeded in bringing us round with a bucket of cold water.

'This isn't good enough,' he said, 'It's the second time you're late.'

The next day, I had an argument with an officer and was fined. We were going around in a vodka haze, 'We'll have to pull ourselves together,' we told each other. 'This is a cushy job.'

We carried out our duties properly for the next two days, but by then the skipper knew he had a couple of no-hopers. However, on the sixth day, an official Russian car pulled up and a splendidly uniformed Russian Naval officer came on board, accompanied by a civilian interpreter. The mate came to see us with a puzzled expression on his face. 'You're to go to the Captain's cabin.'

'Christ, what have we done this time?' Neither of us could recall any new misdemeanour.

In the cabin, the captain and the two men were standing. They both shook hands with us. The interpreter asked if we were William Linskey and Patrick Shaughnessy. The gold uniform then started on a long speech, relayed by the interpreter. Apparently, not only were we heroes, but we'd shown wonderful co-operation with the citizens of Archangel. The spirit of comradeship burned in our breasts, and they appreciated our solidarity with the aims of the Soviet Union. The fight against Fascism came into it and the brotherhood of the world proletariat.

I thought the Captain was going to vomit; his face was a study.

The parting words were a promise: 'This example of valour and friendship will be recorded.'

Final handshakes all round, and they left. The Captain was quiet for a few minutes with a bemused expression on his face.

'I'm trying to imagine what two useless tykes like you could have done to merit the eternal gratitude of the Soviet Union. What happened?'

'I rescued a dog,' said Pat.

The skipper's eyes went up to the ceiling. 'And what did you do?' he asked me.

'During that fire bomb attack, we helped a few people,' I said, 'It's all a bit hazy.'

'Obviously you were drunk,' he said. 'I find it difficult to believe that either of you could do anything useful.'

'What was it all about?' I asked.

He waved his hand and said, 'All to the good, I suppose. All to the good.'

Whatever that meant. Information eventually filtered down that we had been slated to receive a medal, but that the Service had put the block on it as our behaviour made a mockery of the whole thing. That may well have been true; the Russians loved giving medals. Good bye medal.

Chapter 14
Terra Firma

After the visit of the Soviet officials, we behaved reasonably well for a couple of weeks, except for arriving late on a couple of watches and taking the odd jar of marmalade to sell. But as usual Fate gave our tranquillity a nudge. A memo came round that the War Office had decided that we were 'On Active Service' and were therefore entitled forthwith to an allocation of NAAFI rations. This decree would prove to be our downfall.

A little tin of butter or a tin of sardines would sell for 100 roubles. We could always get a few clothes from the Seaman's Mission, and of course on the ship we had our slops—a ration of tobacco, sweets, soap, and cigarettes we were permitted—all of which had enormous trading value. Now a veritable Aladdin's cave opened to us. Scented soap, chocolates, cans of beer, cigarette papers. Cigarette papers were particularly valuable; they could be sold three at a time, because all the old men smoked a foul smelling shag tobacco, which they wrapped in newspaper. What nylon stockings were to Englishwomen, cigarette papers were to Russian men. For a small packet, you'd make a friend for life. I asked one old fellow what was in the news, and he said that he never read it—he only bought it to wrap his fags in.

Naturally the Russian spivs were schemers too. They would pass off any piece of paper that had figures like 100 or 1000 on it as roubles—a used train ticket for example— and I think they even used to print bits of paper with numbers like play money. In fact, even real roubles seemed like play money; I'd never had so many bank notes in my life, but they were bloody useless to accumulate except for buying vodka. There were no jolly souvenirs except perhaps for the carved wooden dolls.

The NAAFI stuff came into the store tax free, and we signed for it to be taken off our pay that we never saw. They started issuing at 10.30 am, when we bought our rations of whiskey, rum, and beer, as well as the rations of men who didn't drink. Neither Pat nor I smoked, and so John and a few of his young mates exchanged their liquor rations for sweets or cigarettes. We started drinking in the focs'le immediately and got very drunk. When our watch was due, we said bollocks, bugger off, and just kept drinking. I'm sure we must have been thoroughly objectionable, but mercifully I can't remember. We didn't work next shift either. Instead, we went ashore, where we stayed for two days until we ran out of the booze. Then we returned to the ship and retrieved the few things we had in our lockers. There wasn't much apart from soap, tobacco, and cigarette papers, and these we sold so as to have plenty of vodka. It was a massive alcoholic binge, about which I have very little recall.

When we eventually returned to the Bard, we were more or less sober. The Captain wanted to see us immediately. 'You, Linskey. I'm discharging you.' To Pat: 'I'll give you another chance.'

Pat said, 'I don't want another chance. If he goes, I go.'

Skipper, 'You'll turn to and go to your watch.' To me. 'You. Tomorrow morning, you'll go to Archangel.'

'Where am I going?'

'You'll find out tomorrow.'

'Bugger this,' said Pat, 'I'm not going to work.'

'You think about it,' said the Captain.

By this time, all the convoy cargoes had been discharged, so they didn't need as many crew. Most of the men were going on day watches, and Pat could have had an easy time. He didn't bother to go on watch, though.

The guard had been told not to let me off the ship. I was a bit sorry about losing such a soft job, but not in the least concerned about my situation. Being a twenty-one-year-old in a foreign land was probably bad enough, but this was a foreign land where I couldn't read a street sign or understand any but a few words—the Cyrillic alphabet was totally incomprehensible to me. Never mind, I had complete confidence that something would turn up. It always did.

The next morning, a peculiarly clad officer turned up for me. He wore an Army battle jacket with army pips and a naval cap. He must have been Combined Operations or Intelligence; if he was an example of what was to come, we were in for a bad time. He was a pompous, arrogant prick, which neither worried nor impressed me.

'Where are we going?' I asked. I'd collected a few things that might come in handy, soap, cigarettes, etc.

Through his stiff upper lip he managed to say: 'I'm taking you to *Intourist*, where you will be accommodated.'

That was promising; by this time *Intourist* felt like home. We went there by ferry; Archangel was getting quiet now, and the weather was turning much colder. Already I was glad of my Airmen's jacket. The officer booked me in; this time I didn't have to share a room.

'You'll hear from us in due course,' Pompous told me. 'Commander Miller may want to interview you. You'll go out on the first available ship.'

Commander Miller was the Chief Legation officer, but of course he didn't bother to get in touch. I was a drunken nuisance, no more.

In a day or two, I met some American naval ratings who were gunners on the *Ironclad*, a ship that had survived the notorious QP17 convoy. Actually they survived it by losing it the sailors said.

I was in the restaurant of the International Club. They'd had a supply in that morning and I was making sure of my share. Three American sailors sat down at my table.

'Gee, they've got vodka,' one said excitedly.

'Not for long, the way it's going,' I replied mournfully.

By now, I knew all the staff. Our current waiter was called Baldy. He came over and bared his teeth in what was intended to be a smile. He was my favourite waiter and often talked to me for as long as ten minutes. It didn't worry him that I couldn't understand him.

It didn't worry me either, as long as he was bringing me vodka.

The first Russian sentence I ever learned was: '*Shto vam ooggodna?*' (What do you want?)

'Four vodkas please.'

'They arrived. In ten minutes, a refill came. But the next order brought forth the second Russian sentence I had learned: '*Vodka nyet.*'

Baldy's expression was always sad when he said this, but then he cheered up a little. '*Mozjet beet zaftra*' (Maybe tomorrow).

The Yanks were really impressed with my linguistic abilities. I was quite proud myself.

'Boy, you sure do have an *in* here,' said one of my new friends, Joe, a small dark Italian American. 'You don't happen to know where there's any coffee, do you?'

'Christ, I'd give my teeth for a cup of coffee,' said another called Abe.

'Why?' I hated coffee, at least what passed for it in England.

'We've been on that effing ship so long we've run out. We can't get any for another week or so.'

'I might be able to get you some. Are there any English ships docked near the *Ironclad*?'

'Yeah, we gotta couple of Limeys there.'

'Then let's go.'

At the docks the guard let me through on my old identity card. In the galley on every English ship I'd sailed on, there had been a large bin full of powdered coffee. This ship was no exception.

'Can I buy some coffee?' I asked the cook.

'You can have the fucking lot if you've got something to carry it in.'

'I'll pay you 500 roubles.'

His eyes lit up. 'Just a minute, I'll find you a tin.' He came back with two tins the size of gallon petrol cans and even filled them up for me.

'I'd better carry them ashore. You just look as though you're helping me. They're used to me going in and out with things.'

The Americans were really grateful. 'I think it must be bloody awful,' I warned, 'I've never seen an Englishman drink it.'

'It'll be wonderful,' they assured me. They took me aboard the *Ironclad* and gave the coffee to the chef. All ranks shared the same mess and the same food. It was the most informal ship's atmosphere I'd ever been in. When the word got out, a lot of the caffeine starved crew came in.

I thought, 'Jesus, when they taste this bloody stuff they'll throw me overboard.' But they all seemed to enjoy it, and every sailor was my friend.

'What's your story?' one asked.

I told them about being fired and sent back to England in the next day or so.

'Do you want a job?'

'Yeah.'

'What do you do?'

'Fireman.'

'A steamship shoveller; we're an oil burner. But there are two jobs going, and one of them is for a wiper in the engine room, I think.'

That'd do me. I was prepared to pretend to be an engineer if it came to it.

The captain, a southerner, looked very old and quite decrepit to my young eyes. I think he must have been let back on a merchant ship because of the shortage of experienced men in the war.

'What job do ye do, boy?'

'Fireman as a rule, but anything below.'

'Well, I need a wiper.'

'I'd like that.' I meant it. I liked everything about this ship.

'Okay boy. Just a minute, what the hell are you doing in Russia, boy?'

My friend told him I'd been fired from my ship. That's buggered my chances, I thought, but the Skipper didn't take any notice. He opened his desk and displayed a bloody great handgun; it was really heavy and about twelve inches long. My Aunt Nellie would have loved it. She could have filled Boot Hill, the cowboy graveyard.

I was glad when he left it there, though, and pulled out some forms. 'What are you, boy, British, Russian, Australian?'

'British.' I signed the papers; it was all very informal.

'Report to the engineer at 9:00 am tomorrow in the engine room. Your wages are $185 a month, plus port bonuses.'

My friend said, 'You've no bloody chance of getting port bonuses on this ship. Forget it. This bastard will never get out of this port.'

I didn't know or care what he was talking about; right now all I knew was that the pay was more than double the British Merchant Navy plus the port bonuses, which turned out to be sums of money given every time the ship moved to a different port. I was a little perplexed by this, as I thought that was why we were on ships—to make them move from one port to another.

Next morning, I went down to the engine room. I'd already met the engineer over coffee the day before. He said, 'Just give those pipes a bit of a rub down; there's nothing really to do.' Not a 'make-work-for-idle-hands man,' evidently. I buggered about, wiping bits and then at 11:00 he told me to go.

The Ironclad was docked at Salumbla, so I took a train to Archangel, where I went to the *Intourist* restaurant and found Pat. 'I've been looking all over for you,' he said.

'What happened?'

'I got fired too. I refused to work.'

He hadn't been given a gold escort like me, though—they'd packed his bag, thrown it onto the dock, and told him to piss off.

'Anyway, I'm out of that.'

I appreciated his loyalty and only hoped he wouldn't regret it.

'What's your news?' he asked.

'I've got a job on an American ship.'

'*Already*?'

'I think I can get you one too.'

'What again?'

I laughed. 'This should be okay. They need a couple of hands.'

'That'll be great.'

'We'd better get back there. I'll introduce you to the skipper.'

Back we went to *The Ironclad*. The guard was so used to the Americans passing that he didn't even bother to come out of his hut. I took Pat aboard. 'Say you're a deckhand,' I warned.

'What do they do?'

'I don't know; you'll have to find out. The sailors reckon the ship will never go to sea anyway.'

The captain was in his cabin. I never saw him anywhere else actually.

'I've brought another friend who needs a job. He's deck crew.'

The old man said, 'I need an able seaman and a quartermaster.'

'I'm a quartermaster,' said Pat.

'Good, Good.' The captain went through the same procedure as yesterday. Pat's eyes popped out at the sight of the gun.

'See the First mate tomorrow.' To me: 'You can show him to quarters.'

A few days later when Pat and I were having a drink by ourselves, I said, 'Pat, do you know that the quartermaster is supposed to be the main man on the deck apart from the bosun?'

'Yes, of course I know.'

'Do you know how to steer?'

'There's nothing to it. I used to watch them on that Danish ship I was on coming back from the States.'

I took him down and introduced him to the friendly crew. We both fitted in immediately. I can remember Slim, Tex, and an elderly man with a bent leg called Gimpy; there were also an escaping Estonian, a Portuguese called De Vlies, and Chico, a typecast Puerto Rican with a pencil thin moustache who talked only about women. There was a young lad about our age from South Carolina; the crew used to tease him by calling him a Cracker and saying he was still fighting the Civil War. Last and most important, was the ship's lawyer, who was named Buster and used to pontificate upon different union rules. Most of his sentences started: 'We can demand, as American seamen . . . .'

We'd been issued with warm clothes and for once common sense prevailed and we hung onto them. We had a ship to live in, with meals guaranteed and more pay than we'd ever earned in our lives.

Pat and I went ashore feeling great. I'd kept the room at *Intourist*—why not, I wasn't paying for it. No one seemed to have been looking for me. Many of the convoy had pushed off from the docks and were anchored in the river ready to move soon.

Life was calm and enjoyable for about ten days. There was very little discipline on *The Ironclad*, and we did little work. The drinkers went ashore, and the others did whatever seamen who don't drink do with their time. The engine room only needed one man to keep it going and we took turns. Nobody cared if any seamen missed their watch; we all fitted in. They were great shipmates.

During this lull, I asked the sceptical naval gunner to explain his snide comments about *The Ironclad* never getting out of port. He said she'd been trying to do this one trip to Russia since just after the U.S. came into the war. She started from Charleston with half the crew made up of American merchant seamen and the other half recruited from jail. The ex-cons must have thought it would be better than serving their sentences, but they'd change their minds about that later. The ship headed for Reykjavik. There were a great number of mishaps from the day they left, so they returned to Halifax. On the second attempt they reached Oban in Western Scotland, where they picked up another convoy to Reykjavik on March 26th 1942. They left Reykjavik for Murmansk on April 8th, but turned back because of bad weather. Some kind of trouble kept them in Iceland for weeks. Having missed a couple of convoys, they set out again but then there was a mutiny, and they had to return to Reykjavik with the homeward bound PQ10. Six mutineers were arrested and flung into jail at the American base. I like to think of the Captain in his cabin repelling the mutineers with his pistol, but I don't think that's what happened. *The Ironclad* picked up three Icelanders as replacements, but the crew was still short-handed. These Icelanders made a brew of moonshine, based on anti-freeze alcohol and fruit juice that drove the crew slightly batty but enabled them to withstand the German onslaught with a degree of fortitude.

With the kind of luck *The Ironclad* had, it wasn't surprising that the next convoy they joined was the ill-fated PQ17. They were meant for each other. At one point, the escort was sent away to fight a non-existent battle, and the merchantmen were left to their own devices. Then the *Ironclad* managed to get lost, which probably saved it from being blown up as so many of the PQ17 were. Instead of going to Archangel, they'd roamed around the Arctic Circle for some time; they turned up safely in Archangel two weeks after the tattered remnants of the PQ17 convoy had limped in.

'I told you there'd be no port bonuses with this tub,' the naval gunner said.

'I'll tell you something else,' put in his mate. 'This ship will never leave Russia. The Russians will probably take it over and call it the *Linskey*.' That was his little joke, but part of it turned out to be prophetic.

'That's right. This ship ain't going nowhere. I wouldn't be surprised if the Skipper gets put in the penitentiary in the U.S.'

'He deserves it. We'd have been off like jackrabbits if we hadn't been in the regular navy. They'd shoot us for desertion if they caught us.'

Under wartime regulations the Skipper could have been jailed for negligence. The ship was so unprepared, it failed to join three different convoys, and then lost its way in the PQ17convoy. Also, liquor was forbidden on American ships, and he drank. Later he was unable to take a course out of the White Sea without running aground. All these mistakes were put down to the Captain. I hoped the crew were wrong, I liked him. In fact, I thought that he was incompetent because he was too old.

Eventually, though, *The Ironclad* pulled out from the dock, down the river, and into the White Sea with the convoy. Pat did two watches without incident, so I came to believe he could steer after all. We were a light ship, as the Russians didn't have any export wood on it. Our position was on the outer, northern row of the convoy. The temperature had dropped right down and a bad storm was blowing. The ship was shuddering and rolling, and the decks were covered in snow. It was the 17th November.

Suddenly there was an awful growling, ripping sound, and we stopped. I came out of the engine room to find men running round the deck shouting, 'What's happened?'

'Don't know.'

I was a bit nervous, but at least the ship wasn't sinking.

'We've hit the rocks.'

What bloody rubbish, I thought. How in hell can we hit rocks in the middle of the White Sea?

They were right, though. The night was black, the wind bit cold, and the waves were breaking hard against the ship. But it held firm; nothing was going to move this baby easily. Pat had been on the bridge and later told us that the ship was in the outside line of the convoy. For the last two days, its course had been fractionally wrong, but with the storm and the small convoy, the escort vessels couldn't have noticed. By the time the storm was really fierce and visibility nil, the *Ironclad*'s course was north instead of west, and it hit the mainland coast.

After about an hour, a British destroyer hove to and hailed us through the loudspeakers: 'What damage?'

'Don't know, can't see, too dark. Taking water, but not sinking. Ship settled on bottom.' That was nice to know.

Destroyer: 'We'll try to tow you off.'

Ironclad: 'No you won't. We'll fill and sink.'

Destroyer: 'We'll have to go then. Will send help.'

At about 10:00 am, it got light but all we could see were big white mountains, absolutely desolate. There was no sign of a building, tree or shrub—just deep snow. It was bloody freezing.

Our escaping Estonian was desolate. 'If we are sent back to Russia, I will never get away. This is my only chance. I thought I had escaped.'

A barge-like ship equipped to pump out water arrived. It was Russian but had a British interpreter on board. They started to pump the hold, but the water came back in just as quickly. Then it was decided that they would keep a skeleton crew on the ship and send the rest back to Archangel. The Estonian was the first volunteer to stay; I suppose he figured that the longer he could remain on board the more chance he had of getting to America. Had we known what our return journey to Archangel was going to be like, they'd have had a full crew sitting in the middle of the White Sea until the war ended.

The next day, a small Russian trawler arrived and took twenty-four men aboard. It was then we learned what discomfort really was. 'Where do we sleep?' asked an American deckhand. The Russian looked at his sleeping motions and sneered. Pat and I realised that there was nowhere even to sit. We found a small bathroom with a bit of floor space. Gimpy came along too, and we commandeered what proved to be the prime site. It had an iron deck floor to lie on and there was a shower that constantly dripped and never drained—in the rough sea, the water sloshed higher and higher wetting all the floor. It was freezing; the cold was unbelievable. The other men huddled in any sheltered spot they could find.

There was no sign of food to warm us. One American made eating signs that he was hungry and the Russian said 'Tojya.'

'What did he say?' the Yank asked me.

'Also.'

They really didn't have any food themselves. I never saw a Russian eat any more than a crust of black bread during the whole trip. It had taken two days to get there, but the small slow ship took four dreadful days to get back. In comparison, the seven days in the open lifeboat in the Atlantic had been a holiday cruise. Once a day we got a cup of hot water, which I found very welcome. One American said, 'I'd give anything for a cup of coffee. The bastards threatened to put a tea bag in this water.'

The young cracker lad said wonderingly, 'I have never before in my whole life felt hunger. I didn't know what it was. I swear to God I'll never pass a bum without giving him a handout for the rest of my life.'

An older sailor said, 'You'd better keep your head down, kid. You're probably the tenderest meat around.'

Buster, the sea lawyer, was in his element. 'I tell you this. We can demand first class transport—'

'Shut your fucking mouth, you stupid bastard, 'said a naval rating. 'This IS first class transport for Archangel.'

'I'm speaking on behalf of the Mercantile Marine.'

Someone muttered, 'I wish the fucking Statue of Liberty would loom for *us* huddled bloody masses.'

'We'll be sitting out the rest of the war in Archangel,' said our prophetic naval friend.

'Have you got any more good ideas, Bill?' asked Pat.

However, the nightmare of hunger and exposure finally ended, as all nightmares do. Back we went to the mouth of the River Dvina, this time to a small town called Molotovsk, which was a submarine base. An American official took us to wooden barracks, where the small rooms held two bunks. We sat down to an enormous meal. We were all so busy eating that we didn't speak until coffee was the only thing left in front of us. Then the Cracker lad said, 'I wonder if those poor Russian crewmen got food?' A charity worker had been born, but I don't think he survived the trip home.

They issued us with good warm clothes, and I went to have a hot bath. I carefully checked that toes, fingers, and all other hanging extremities were still intact, as I hadn't felt them for five days.

I thought I'd sleep for a week but the smell of bacon and eggs woke me.

Chapter 15
Black Market.

The gunner prophet was absolutely right: the *Ironclad* never did leave. It was salvaged by the Russians and renamed not *Linskey* but *Marina Raskova.* I don't know about the Skipper's fate. Another American ship had run aground that night too. It was rumoured that the crew was going to stay on and be towed back, but that the American Captain had said the equivalent of 'Bollocks' and demanded all his crew be sent home. Eventually, the Americans abandoned the ship and the Soviets salvaged it. That crew must have had their own ship's lawyer like Buster.

We were all put on the PX list, which was the American equivalent of the duty free NAAFI. We could now buy food, chocolates, booze and soap, as well as getting a good exchange rate for all the currency we needed. Of course, we were still on crew pay—American ship owners didn't stop it like the English did.

Two of the lads said, 'Tonight we're going up to the Snake Ranch.'

'What's that?'

'It's a great place. These women have been sent here from all over Russia to work in the docks or timber yards or factories. They're like us, lonely as hell. We're always welcome.'

The Americans' randy reputation made us think they were talking about a brothel, but a few days later we met some Norwegian seamen in the village. 'That's the Snake Ranch,' they told us. 'Those women aren't whores; they may come across sometimes, but they're just lonely. There aren't any Russian men about.'

'How do we get initiated?'

'Take a bottle and knock on any door. You'll be welcomed. In the evening, of course; they're working now.'

It was true. I made a lot of friends there, and it was the Snake Ranch that probably helped me hold onto a vestige of my sanity. I also started learning Russian properly there in the time-honoured way—in bed.

Through the walls, you might hear the odd sailor trying to get one of the girls to come across with what they called 'Home Comforts.'

A tin was slapped down on the table. 'There, a can of butter?'

'*Nyet.*' Absolutely unyielding.

Another bang on the table. 'And a tin of beans?'

'*Nyet.*' No softening.

'And a tin of Spam?' (Sailor becoming despondent.)

A moment's pause for thought, then a slightly weakened '*Nyet.*'

Pleadingly: 'Well here, honey. A nice big bar of chocolate.'

'*Mmm. Da. Kharashore.*' Deal done, both parties happy.

The Russian women were wonderful; they treated us as part of the families they missed so much. There were about sixty of them in the Snake Ranch and they adopted us. They taught us Russian words and were so pleased that someone wanted to learn their language. I discovered much later that this was the sort of language you learn on the street and never in a classroom, but it gave us a fluency that a student would never hear. I think the first and most useful word that I learned was *Blat*, which meant graft or a pay off; it was in constant use. In the beginning, we just built up a vocabulary of words with no grammar. Then we managed to buy an English primer for Russian speakers and by reversing everything we learned the Cyrillic alphabet. Then it was like playing charades. Russian women would come up and ask for what sounded like *odeyalo,* putting two hands together by their ears in the gesture for sleep. After we'd been through night-dresses and sheets, we'd eventually come to blankets. *Da Da,* that was it. I would never forget words learned in this way. *Zaftra* (tomorrow) was probably the second word I learned, which they used more often than the Spanish use mañana.

The term *Politzia* for the police had been obliterated from the language, because it dated from the hated Czarist regime. The *Militia,* however, were everywhere— they were only cops by a different name. On the surface, everyone and everything was strictly regimented; you had to pull out identity papers or some bloody paper every five minutes, worse than back in England. Even a twenty-mile train journey needed permission, your identity card, and of course a ticket. Under this official surface, though, every form, billet or document could be obtained for *Blat.* The Russians survived by sheer cunning and many became masters at forgery. At the same time, however, the *Militia*'s attitude was that if the paper was the right colour and had an official stamp, they would pass it and make life easier for themselves.

All the small villages for twenty or thirty miles around had little markets which sprang up on street corners wherever anyone had something to sell. While the laws were clear—goods were not to be sold and it was a criminal offence to make a profit—the *Militia* on duty didn't want to be bothered with petty arrests and gave the traders plenty of warning to bugger off. Every so often, though, one of the worst offenders would spend some time in jail.

Although there was a real fear of the Gulags, anarchy prevailed under the surface, for this was the only way the Russians could stay alive. When glasnost and perestroika came, the criminal form that capitalism took came as no surprise to those who knew the country. Russians had been told for seventy years that capitalists were criminals—why would they not follow that example?

The crew of the *Ironclad* was to be repatriated, Pat and I with them if we wanted to go. I was in two minds, but Pat wanted to go home. He was only eighteen and he wanted to see his family. We decided to be paid off and stay in Archangel until the convoys started again. We should have gone then.

Buster came into his own. He said the crew was getting the first class accommodation they were entitled to. He told us we couldn't get money in Russia and would have to go to Waterman Shipping, the shipping company in England which dealt for the owners. If the Skipper just gave us an unendorsed check, it would be useless; no one would pay out. He told us to get the Naval Attaché down to the ship to stamp and endorse the check at the same time as the Captain. We did and they also signed a declaration to Waterman's Steamship Company. Then Buster asked one of the sailors to make a waterproof belt for each of us, to be worn next to the body. If we were unlucky enough to go into the drink again, it would keep the papers dry.

After they'd all left, the quarters were closed down and the whole place became desolate. We lost our access to the PX too, which was really a blow. So we went back to *Intourist*, which felt like home. It was winter now and the weather had got worse—first snow which then froze, then more snow and more freezing, a process which repeated itself too many times. Along the pavements, the snow lay seven to eight feet deep and passages had to be cut for pedestrians to walk. The ferry stopped running, and within a week the river was solid enough for cars to drive across. A roadway formed across the ice and eventually big trucks were going over. Inside the houses and hotels it was warm, for with all the timber in the area there was no shortage of wood, thank God.

Human beings became round bundles. Some had decent boots, but many had to stuff newspaper in their shoes and inside clothing to make extra layers of insulation. Girls we had known as pretty little doll-like creatures became unrecognisable and unattractive. Who wanted to know in temperatures of forty-five below zero?

There was still an Airforce base and sometimes we could go there and get blankets and cigarettes or tobacco. We would take our goods to small towns where we knew they had vodka and trade. But sometimes we went hungry—quite often in fact—and for once food became more important than drink. Even fish, beetroot, and cabbage soup became quite tasty. I never actually enjoyed it, but I was certainly glad to eat it. When we had money, we used to have *Kasha* (porridge), black bread, and caviar for breakfast at *Intourist*. That's the only part of wartime Russian cuisine I'd ever like to have again.

After a couple of weeks, the desk at *Intourist* told us that two men had come looking for us. As no ships were going anywhere, we realised we'd be held in custody until the convoys started again if they found us. So we packed our bags with the belongings we'd accumulated, and went back to the Snake Ranch at Molotovsk. The girls moved us around to different rooms all the time for safety.

And then I fell in love.

I had already been introduced to Galya, but at the time she was just this bundle in the street—there could have been a bear under all the clothes, and I guess I was a bit offhand. Then a dance was held where I saw a vision with a beautiful figure, high Slavic cheekbones, and green eyes like a cat. But she nodded to me very coldly, which wasn't the normal reaction of girls.

'I'm sorry, have we met before?' I asked. I had enough Russian by now to blunder through a sentence.

She said we had and made it fairly obvious that it wasn't an experience she wanted particularly to repeat. Not only did I have to woo her but also her strict parents; she was seventeen and still lived with them. I'd had my first sexual experience at the age of fourteen in the outdoor washhouse. Much of the Tyneside population was probably conceived in washhouses; using them only on a Monday had seemed wasteful, so the Jarrow youngsters did their best to utilise their amenities.

But Galya was different. She was my first real love, and she seemed so exotic and romantic, I didn't dream of having the sort of slap and tickle we'd all indulged in at home. Instead, I smuggled my sexual desires into the Snake Pit, while Galya cosseted my spiritual ones. This was romance as far as I was concerned and my intentions were serious. Galya was the gentlest girl I had ever met, and I treated her like a piece of porcelain. I was really a bit embarrassed by the strength of my feelings. I went to visit her one day and she played the balalaika and sang a Russian love song to me. Pat came in and shook his head in disbelief to see me felled by a pair of beautiful eyes.

Pat made up a foursome with another girl called Tamara, who was Galya's cousin. When the weather permitted, we went for long walks together, and eventually we became welcome in their homes. Like all the Russians I met, these families were most hospitable; Russian men enjoyed enthusiastic drinking in common with the Irish, and we used to drink vodka with Galya's father. We were still drinking much too much; a bottle of vodka a day had become habit.

One day her father spoke to me and without first having to translate in my mind I understood him. Then I replied. Her father said, 'Now you can speak our language.' It was true; I could speak and understand it. It made such a change to my feeling about myself. All my life the authorities had been telling me what a mindless fool I was, so I'd lived up to that reputation. Now I could do something all these pompous bastards couldn't.

There wasn't much in the way of vulgar entertainment in Archangel, but we used to go to dances at Intourist, and there were many concerts at the International Club. Sometimes a solo pianist played, and once a thirty-piece orchestra and several singers. Occasionally they showed a film. I remember seeing *The Battleship Potemkin* twice, as well as Disney cartoons.

We heard there would be a convoy in March. There were about six Allied ships in Archangel and apparently a whole convoy in Murmansk. They were going to bring in an icebreaker to allow the Archangel ships to join the rest. The sea never froze over there; it was just here in the Dvina River and the White Sea that we were icebound.

'What do you think about taking it?' I asked Pat.

'I've had enough, I'd like to get home. The family must think I'm dead,' he said. 'I don't want to live through another winter like this, do you?'

'Christ, no. I want to marry Galya. I'll have to get everything aboveboard before I'll be able to get permission.'

So we went and surrendered to Commander Miller at Norway House. Dressed in Naval Commander's uniform, he came out to the reception area very quickly and stood looking at us with a quizzical expression.

'At last. You're Linskey and Shaughnessy.'

He seemed an agreeable sort of person, aged about fifty; he didn't appear to be angry, just curious. 'As a result of your disappearances, reported sightings and wanderings, I've had more trouble and work than I've had with the war. There is a desk full of cable messages and radio inquiries from London, asking your whereabouts and how you could disappear in the Soviet Union with all their restrictions on movement. I'm rather curious myself. However, I'm not going to lecture you or ask where you've been because it's a waste of time, and it would serve no purpose. I suppose I should hold you, but I can't be bothered. I'll send you back to the *Intourist* and put you on the first convoy back to the UK. If you miss it, you can stay in Russia for the rest of your lives as far as I'm concerned. You'll probably end up in Siberia; that would be a short life, although it would feel very long.'

That was it. We left.

'That wasn't too bad, was it? He doesn't seem a bad bloke.' I said to Pat.

'No, but just don't get any more good ideas. Please.'

We thought we'd have to wait at least a month because of the freeze up. However, the convoy was going to leave Murmansk soon, and those ships still in Archangel would quickly have to move out to join it. We were to travel on the *SS Empire Archer*.

We went to The Snake Pit to say thanks and goodbye. After that, we spent all the remaining time with our girlfriends. Pat went off with Tamara and I met Galya. I told her we had to leave the next day. But she must have sensed our departure was imminent; she had brought me some snapshots to put in my wallet.

'I am so unhappy, Beel. I will never see you again.'

'I hope you will darling. I love you so much. If I get another trip, we will get permission to marry. If not, I will certainly be back as soon after the war as I can.'

'But it is so dangerous that you must go back to England now. What if your ship is attacked?'

'If I don't come back for you within a year of the war finishing, you must accept that I have died. I'll write to you, but if you meet someone else, make a life for yourself.'

By that time, we were both very upset. I felt that the lump in my throat would choke me. I would have liked to roar with pain.

We had to meet Pat and Tamara at the International. There was a dance, so I had the opportunity to hold Galya all evening. Neither of us spoke much.

I walked her home. We stood in the hallway for a long time, but I remember nothing we said except 'I love you.' We said goodbye with hugs, kisses, and tears. Then I got on the ship and got plastered with a bottle of vodka. The convoy trailed in the path of the icebreaker. It was an eerie experience; *The Empire Archer* was groaning against the weight of the ice pressing against it. Daylight lasted only for two hours, followed by a peculiar kind of dim light for the other twenty-two. It was like looking through a night scope. There was a deep silence, apart from of the engines and the sound of the ice trying to crush the ship. Millions of stars twinkled in the dusk, but our world was vast, quiet, and empty

Shortly after arriving in Murmansk there was an air raid. Scarcely a day had passed since the convoys started that there had not been one; it was just that bit nearer than Archangel for the planes to travel. The Germans blasted the wooden docks away in the daytime, and the Russians built them back in the night. The city had taken a dreadful battering. During this particular air raid, one of the crew bailed out of a German plane that had been hit, and opened his parachute. As he floated down, he was waving his arms, no doubt hoping to express eternal friendship. An American gunner ignored his pleas and kept a hail of bullets going into his body. The plane didn't disintegrate but fell in the water, where a Russian ship sped through it. That was successful Allied co-operation.

On 1st March 1943, a thirty-ship convoy left the Kola Inlet bound for Loch Ewe. Tankers were prime targets and could not outrun anything, so the funnel of the tanker *Oligarch* was cut down, fitted with a spark arrester, and then disguised with a dummy funnel and superstructure. Apparently this worked well, and a few other tankers in future convoys would adopt the same disguise.

A severe storm blew up, which mercifully I knew little about as I was too busy drinking the vodka we'd brought with us. I was in a bad state; I could hear voices in my head, and I was shaking like a leaf. Pat was in a similar condition, but the delusions were tolerable as long as we had some alcohol. We managed to keep going right through the trip, but I remember little about it.

The convoy had to scatter in the storm, and three ships were sunk by a sub on 5th March. Several others were damaged by the storm on the 8th March and another merchant went to the bottom on 9th. In all, six shops were lost to subs and weather.

We heard that *The Scharnhorst*, a German battleship, had left Gdynia in Poland for Norway. This was a terrible threat to merchant shipping, so our destroyers all left to counter any trouble. We were just lucky that there wasn't a repeat of the PQ17 disaster on 7th July, 1942—the worst of the war to date— when two-thirds of the convoy was lost.

Our convoy of twenty-six ships arrived in Loch Ewe in various states of disrepair on 14th March. The storm was appalling. Even in harbour, sheets of rain hid almost everything from sight, although we could hear the crew's shouts of panic as the rocks came closer. Our ship, *The Empire Archer*, had her anchor down, but it was inadequate. It didn't stop us being pulled along the sea bed towards the rocks. Then the anchor struck something, and we ground to a stop. It was pure luck.

We were supposed to go around the north of Scotland—back to Newcastle probably—but Pat and I demanded they let us off there in Loch Ewe; one shipwreck had been enough for us. The captain said he understood our feelings, but it was so rough that no boat would consider setting sail for the mainland. However, he promised that if the weather improved next day, he would see that we landed.

It did. A bus took us to a debriefing by Intelligence Officers in the small town of Aultbea, which had been turned into a Ministry of Defence headquarters with the whole area fenced off from civilians. They soon realised I had no knowledge of anything military, but they were quite impressed by my fluency in Russian, which pleased me.

We were put on a bus. Our fellow passengers were English-speaking Russians, embassy replacements who had also decided to get off the convoy. Once outside the restricted area, we picked up two local passengers at a farm; when they started speaking, the Russians looked amazed. I couldn't understand a word of Scots Gaelic either, but I recognised it from my childhood and told them it was only used in the Highlands in Scotland.

We went to Edinburgh on a small local railway line from Achnasheen. There was a two-hour wait for the train to Newcastle, so we had a drink in the buffet. Pat thought it was odd— considering he was on the way home, he felt quite depressed. So did I.

In mid-March all Russian convoys were suspended, because the German Battleships, the *Tirpitz,* the *Scharnhorst* and the *Lutzow,* were based in Northern Norway. With twenty-three hours of light each day in summer, any allied shipping would have been annihilated. The next convoy was to be in December 1943.

I missed Galya terribly. She'd given me the first love and tenderness since my mother died. But all the letters I wrote sat somewhere in England for these nine months and when the war was over, Churchill made his 'Iron Curtain' speech closing all corridors of communication and beginning the 'Cold War.'

I never saw her again.

PART FOUR :

SERVICES NO LONGER REQUIRED

Chapter 16

Welcome the sailor?

When we arrived in Jarrow, we went first to Pat's place, where his several little sisters and stepbrother were all over us. It felt so civilized to have a small body snuggling in to be told a story or teased. Up to a month before our return, our families had believed we were dead.

Pat's father, Marty, told me: 'Your father couldn't keep the house up by himself, Bill. He's living with your Aunt Nellie.'

'She'll have a full house then. I'll stop by Mima's and see if she can put me up.'

My cousin John had come back from Russia on the same convoy. He'd changed from a boy into a man, even though he was still only seventeen. 'It was wonderful,' he said. 'Thanks for helping me get there, Bill. I'm not going to sea again, though. I have a year before I'm called up, so I'm going to get all the education I can.'

'That's a good idea.' I said and I meant it.

Mima was so happy to have him back she'd even forgiven me for encouraging him to go in the first place. 'Stay with us here, Billy. You can have the little room to yourself.'

Next I went to my Aunt Nellie's, who told me I should be pistol-whipped for taking 'that young John into heathen places.' Still, she hugged me and cried a little bit. 'We all thought you were dead, Billie.' Da was at the pub, so I went along to see him. He too was moved at seeing me. I began to feel loved again and that I belonged somewhere.

Pat and I had two lots of money to collect. From Newcastle, we had the biggest amount to come from the *Ironclad*'s shipping office; the smaller sum from the *Empire Bard* was to be collected from South Shields. We didn't want to go there until we had to because we'd have to sign on to the Pool again, so next day we went—together with Da—to Newcastle to collect the *Ironclad* money.

We presented our endorsed checks with the Embassy stamps and our credentials, and after a surprising lack of formality left with £200 each clutched in our hands. We looked at each other in awe. We hadn't seen this much money in our lives.

At that time you could buy a house in Jarrow for about £90. British seamen's wages were now £11 a month, so we had about eighteen months' wages each.

'Let's get a drink and a really good meal.'

We went to a good restaurant in Newcastle. If you had money, there were good meals to be found despite food rationing. We had thick barley soup, Scotch salmon and a steak. We looked so disreputable that the HeadWaiter came up to tell us how much it would be before we started—about twenty pounds for the three of us. It was the first time in my life I ever left a tip.

I was on top of the world. **Rich!!** I didn't believe I could spend that much money in my lifetime. Considering the next two days cost another £25 I should have adjusted that to a very short lifetime.

My father said, 'You're both looking really scruffy. Why don't you go and buy some new clothes?'

'There's plenty of time for that Da. Let's have a drink.'

I gave him a bundle of money and after a quick drink he left. He didn't want to get involved in what would probably turn into a binge.

'Seriously Pat, we've got enough money here to start a business. We'd never have to work for anyone else again.'

He agreed. 'Let's do that. I think right now though we'll have to buy our mates a drink.'

'Of course we do.'

So a serious few days drinking started, which cost us each another ten percent of our fortune.

Then something rather odd happened. I began to hear a brass band playing.

'What are you doing, Billie?'

'I'm listening to the band. I like that tune!'

'I can't hear anything.'

Poor deaf buggers, I thought. Then voices would start whispering to me when I was alone, but I didn't tell anyone in case they thought there was something wrong with my head. After a while, I heard someone murmur about someone else being bomb happy. I hoped it wasn't Pat—it couldn't have been me. I was okay, just a bit tired.

Our shoes started wearing out, but we didn't feel like spending our money on clothes. Every time we had in the past they'd got lost. Maybe if we didn't have new clothes we wouldn't be torpedoed again. So we went to a Distressed Seamen's Help place. We got underwear, shoes, socks and shirts to fit, but outerwear was more of a problem. All available pants were narrow, almost stovepipe, in a world where the fashion was for wide-legged trousers. Only two jackets fitted us, because we both had massive shoulders from shoveling coal. Mine was a gamekeeper's jacket with pockets all over the place for ferret or rabbit carrying, I suppose. Pat's was more like a Cinema Usher's jacket with lots of buttons. We decided they'd do—we could cover them up with our reversible raincoats. As these raincoats were identical, we agreed to take turns which side to wear so we didn't look ridiculous.

The first time we appeared in the pub clad in these rig-outs we caused gales of laughter. 'You look like a pair of bloody clowns,' said both our fathers.

'Why waste money? They'll only be bloody blown up,' we said.

I wasn't feeling very well, though. I told Pat and my friends that I was going to stop drinking for a couple of days. Pat thought was that a great idea; he wasn't feeling too marvelous either.

The main problem was my shadow. He stood just behind my right shoulder and whispered to me. I used to jerk my head around to see him, but he was always too fast. Sometimes I'd try keeping my head looking straight ahead but swiveling my eyes around to the back. I could just see the shadow, but not properly. I decided it must be the Devil.

Although I knew these hallucinations were imagination, they were so vivid that sometimes I really couldn't believe they weren't real.

When the pub shut, I said I'd see them all in three days time; I was off the grog. I went home for a sleep, but something woke me up. Little tiny men jumping on and off the bed had shaken me awake. I told them to piss off, but they just laughed at me. They wanted to play, but I wanted to sleep. Peter, Mima's young lad of about ten, came in to the room.

'You yelled out. What do you want Bill?'

'Just get some cushions, son, and block the side of the bed. Those little men are driving me mad jumping up and down.'

He looked at me a bit anxiously, then peered under the bed. 'I can't see any little men,' he said, but he put the cushions round as I'd asked and I went back to sleep. Not for long though.

Through layers of sleep, I felt eyes staring at me. I opened my own eyes and there, twelve inches away on the bedside table, was a rat. Just looking at me. I let out a shriek and Mima came in.

'What's the matter, love?'

'Rats. You've got rats in the house.' Another one jumped up on the table and started cleaning his whiskers, just like a cat. They were sleek and well fed. I screamed and tried to push them away, but they slid off the table.

Mima came from a long line of Irish alcoholics. She knew what state I was in.

'Go and get your Uncle Tommy,' she ordered young Peter. 'Tell him Billie's got the rats and it's urgent.'

A rat jumped on the bed. I shrieked and kicked it off. Sweat was pouring off me; I was gasping for air, and my heart was trying to break out of my chest.

Mima said, 'Billie, there aren't any rats. You know that they're in your head.'

'You're right,' I said. I did know it somewhere, but another rat jumped on the bed and I screamed and pulled the bedclothes over my head. Tommy arrived and sat beside me. He had been a terrible drunk in his time, but one day he and a friend went to the Catholic Church and signed the Pledge. Plenty of others had signed with the best intentions and never kept the promise, but Tommy and his friend did. They never told a single soul what had happened to them that made them reform. They were both pillars of the community now and had been for years.

'I know exactly what you're going through, Bill. Have you got any drink?'

'I'm not drinking today.'

'That's why you've got the D.T's. You have to have a drink.'

I had half a bottle of whiskey under the bed, and he gave me a little medicine glass. He had also brought a big bottle of pills and made me take about ten of them with water. I think they were Vitamin B. They were hard to swallow, but the rats disappeared and my heart stopped racing. But now there were filthy lice crawling all over me; the rats must have left them behind I had a bath and felt a bit better; then Mima had some soup heated for me and they went away.

'God, that was awful,' I said, after I thanked Tommy.

'You must go to a doctor,' he said. 'You should take the drink a bit easy Bill. Every time you have the D.T.'s your brain gets damaged.'

'Oh, I will,' I assured him. 'I'm never going to drink anything but beer from now on.'

He looked disappointed, but said nothing and left.

I went back to the pub a day early. If I got the rats because I'd stopped drinking, obviously I needed a drink so I wouldn't get them again. It seemed that drink was the medicine, not the cause. I was terrified at the thought of having hallucinations again, but even more of the palpitations. I had thought I was going to die. Unfortunately it only took one beer and the voices started again. I knew a doctor who was a heavy drinker, so I went to see him.

When I told him about the hallucinations, he gave me an injection and a bottle of pills. He told me that I'd get them again if I wasn't careful. His fee was a bottle of whiskey. While I was buying it, I saw Pat and told him about my nasty experience. We had just a couple of pints and arranged to meet tomorrow to discuss going in to a business. On the way home, my shadow reappeared. Now I knew it was the Devil, because he was giving an evil little chuckle and saying, 'You're right in the shit; you're not long for the top.'

Next day over a beer I said, 'What will we invest the money in?'

Pat said, 'What fucking money? Mine's all gone. How much have you got left?'

I had just about five pounds. 'Where's it all gone?' I was dismayed. It wasn't possible to spend that much money in two weeks—was it?

'Yours on the rats,' Pat said, 'Mine probably on someone else's rats.'

We had to go back to the Pool. They owed us money, and we supposed we'd have to go back to sea.

'There's one good thing,' said Pat. 'They reckon that the Allies—that's us—have got the Germans beaten in the Atlantic with some system that can find the subs.'

Maybe the gods would smile on us this time. I didn't really feel well enough to work, but I'd have to. I was so depressed and we were still wearing our ridiculous clothes. Something that's funny if you have plenty of money is just bloody pathetic if you're broke.

Chapter 17.

Adrift on Dry Land.

We went to the Pool in South Shields expecting terrible abuse for not signing in earlier.

The bloke behind the counter was a miserable bugger who was well hated in Jarrow. Before the war, he was the assessor in the Means Test Office. He seemed to be waiting for us; a wintry smile crossed his face when we arrived. He handed me a big brown envelope. Inside was a reckoning of the money due to me with subs and union fees taken out. The remaining pay was only about £11 and of course the regular £13 to replace clothing. That was from the *Empire Beaumont* sinking which felt like several centuries past.

The next page was a list of misdemeanors. Only those since the forming of the wartime Pool, but there were still enough.

5 missed ships

12 drunk and disorderly

AWOL in Virgin Island

6 weeks in jail in London

10 skipped doing day work in port

8 Insubordination

Fired in Russia for drunkenness and absence from work on *The Empire Bard*

Missing three convoys when repatriated to England

10 times late reporting for duty

They didn't mention trying to get into the locked bond; I suppose they couldn't prove it. Other than that, it seemed about normal for a black-crew member. I gave him a puzzled look.

'There's another page.'

So there was; I turned it over: 'Disobeying orders to stay aboard ship and general unsatisfactory conduct.' And then in large letters: **'SERVICES NO LONGER REQUIRED.'**
I was surprised. I couldn't have gone to sea again because my hands trembled and my nerves were shot. From being a healthy young man, I was now, at twenty-two years of age, like a palsied old man. I felt very angry though at being so summarily dismissed. Of course I'd misbehaved, I was a civilian seaman, but also I'd worked through appalling enemy attacks.

'What have you got to say for yourself?' asked the clerk. This really infuriated me.

'I've got fuck all to say to you, you pen-pushing prick. You've never been to sea in your bloody life. Why don't you bugger off and do a bit of work, instead of hiding here in a woman's job?'

They had given Pat a second chance, no doubt thinking I had led him astray. Perhaps I had, but he'd been more than willing. We sat outside to discuss the situation.

'Bill, I think I'd like to take the second chance if you don't mind. I'm nineteen; they'll put me in the Army otherwise.'

'Of course I don't mind. You've got a lot more to see yet.'

I waited while he went back in to find out about his next ship. I didn't mind not going back to sea; I'd had enough. As there weren't any convoys going to Russia again I wouldn't get to see Galya. I'd go on the dole for a while.

Pat went to the U.S on one trip and jumped ship again to stay with his family. He was there about three months and spent most of that time drinking. He had intended to stay in America this time, but he made no effort to look for work. He palled up with Dennis Waters, a cousin of mine, and they roistered through the town. A patrol picked them up at the Seaman's Mission, and they were sent to Ellis Island—the second time for Pat. He thought that he would be in terrible trouble because he had been there before, but they didn't look up his record. After several weeks, the immigration officials found him a berth on a troop ship, which was returning to England.

By now, the might of America's manufacturing capacity had won the battle of the Atlantic and the awful attacks on the convoys came to an end around March 1943. Some ships still went down, but the Americans had brought in superior equipment and more German subs were being sunk instead.

Pity I'd been fired; never mind, something would turn up.

The next few weeks are a bit clouded. I had no money but as long as I was in Jarrow I would never want for a drink. I was popular, because I laughed and fooled about; even now that I drank too much, people still considered me good company.

It didn't take many drinks to set off the DTs, though, and now my hallucinations were worse. I began to be afraid to walk around too, and I couldn't go under railway bridges in case a train went over—the noise was like a bomber coming at me. The Devil was more often at my shoulder, but mostly in the dark. I was afraid to go to sleep because my nightmares always returned. There was still a blackout of course, so the only places with plenty of lights were pubs. One publican gave me a pound every morning to go and drink at another pub, because I upset his customers by shaking so much. And time was becoming very confused. I would go out for a pee in one pub and find myself in a different one on a different day.

I was afraid someone would find out and put me in a lunatic asylum. I was rapidly disintegrating.

People would upset me. I'd get angry and I'd be arrested. The Superintendent of Police was a great big fat man named George Joshua Hammond. All the local drunks, crooks, naughty boys and even his own police force was terrified of him. Several hated him. For some reason, though, he was extremely kind to me. He was the first person who ever suggested that I could keep out of trouble by not drinking.

My cell was fairly big, about seven by ten feet, which left a lot of space. The only furniture was a single bed shelf about two feet off the floor; in the day, this had a wooden pillow, which was covered at night by a soft pillow and a blanket.

The desk sergeant would let Hammond into my cell, where he would lower his large frame onto the wooden bench. Each time the conversation took the same turn.

'Now Bill, the police don't hate you; in fact, a lot of them like you. But you give them no alternative but to arrest you.' Or he would say, 'Now tell me Bill, what trouble have you ever been in when you didn't drink?'

I thought at the time he was nuts—everyone in Jarrow drank. But I had to admit I couldn't remember being in trouble.

'There you see,' he said. 'You're a nice lad when you stay off it.'

I'd go into the local police station and appear before the magistrate the next day. George Joshua Hammond used to sit in the well of the court and tell the magistrate what he knew about the prisoner. For me, he used to plead that I'd had an unfortunate childhood and a bad war. For several weeks he managed to keep me from getting anything worse than fines. One time he stood up for me and said, 'I find this boy is a very sad case.'

The next day the local paper had the headline: 'BAD, SAD OR MAD?'

Of course I never paid the fines. In the end, they all accumulated and I was given six weeks in Durham Jail. When I sobered up after a couple of days I found the routine tolerable. After being used to a ship's watch, it was peaceful to have eight hours sleep and food three times a day. The food wasn't wonderful, but it was often non-existent outside when I was drinking. Best of all were the books, even though there weren't any of the favorite writers of the day like James Cain, Dashiel Hammett or Raymond Chandler. Just classics. I read *Crime and Punishment* and the novels of Charles Dickens. There was a bit of light relief in P.G. Wodehouse. Every prisoner in those days had a cell to himself. I had time to think that there might be an alternative way of living. I felt there was something better if I could only find it.

On the day of my release, I went to the Governor's office. He did a spiel about hoping not to see me again. Then he handed me a paper. It turned out to be a demand that I should attend a medical examination that very day with a view to being conscripted into the Armed Forces. I was absolutely gutted.

The Governor said, 'Service isn't so bad. It will make a man of you.'

'I've been a fucking man in the Merchant Service for five years. What more do they want?'

He looked surprised. 'I didn't know—it's not on your record here. You'll have to attend—this afternoon, isn't it? The police will pick you up otherwise. Get it over with.'

I sat outside in the sun, thinking. Ever since Dunkirk, an army of two million had been sitting on their arses in the UK while the Russians did all the fighting in Europe. And then 140,000 American troops had landed in North Africa in November and paratroopers had dropped in to Morocco and Algiers with little resistance. I wasn't going to kill anyone; in fact it looked as though the Allied Army wasn't going to either. Anyway, the cemeteries in France had their quota of my uncles from the First World War.

What could they do to me? Put me in jail? That would suit me fine.

I was ready for my medical.

I showed the paper to the corporal behind the desk at the Army Recruitment Office. 'Go to room six.'

Two other men were waiting; one was called in before I sat down. The other said nothing, but looked scared to death. When my name was called, I entered this long room, more like a wide corridor. Along each side were four tables with an Army Doctor seated at each. Behind were curtained cubicles. Without looking at me, the first one said, 'Strip off.'

'Bollocks to that. What am I going to strip off for?'

Now he did look at me. 'You've come here for a medical.'

'I haven't asked for a medical.'

'It's for conscription into the Armed services.'

'Fuck the Armed Services.'

He was visibly shaken. 'Why are you so angry?'

'I've just come from four years of being bombed and torpedoed.'

'I'll just take your heartbeat then. You needn't get undressed.'

'Okay.' I let him take it. Then he sent me to the next doctor, who must have heard the preceding interview.

'I only want a blood sample,' he said.

'No needles.'

He sent me to the third one. I think he was a psychiatrist.

'Tell me what the trouble is. Why are you so angry?'

'I've just come out of six weeks in jail. Before that, I spent four years at sea hauling food and ammunition into this bloody country so all the fat petty officials and their fat families could eat. I've been bombed, strafed, torpedoed, shipwrecked, and nearly frozen to death. I've spent seven days in an open boat in the middle of the bloody big Atlantic. Those bastards have told me that my services are no longer required.

'Now *you* want a piece of me. What fucking use can I be to you if those bastards don't want me?'

'There's no need to swear,' he said primly.

'The only way you'll get me in the Army is in a straitjacket. The minute I get it undone, I'll kill the first fucking General I lay eyes on.'

The doctor said, 'All right. Just sit over there and compose yourself for a few minutes.'

He went away with my file and all eight doctors grouped at the far end of the room, consulting. Then an older doctor asked me to come into a small side room. His eyes were kind and he showed no disapproval.

'What were you in prison for, if you don't mind me asking?'

'Ever since I came back from sea I've had a lot of aggravation. I seem to be surrounded by petty officials. Half the time I've got voices in my head telling me to do something. Then the officials are telling me to sign this, go and get buff form so and so, then take it to green window and get a red sticker or some bloody rubbish. So I take a couple of drinks and I get put away. I've had too much of this. I don't want to hear any guns or fire any guns. I won't kill anyone for the bloody army. I just want to be left in peace.'

'Do you hear anything besides voices?'

I was surprised. I didn't think he'd know about that. 'Yes, a band strikes up sometimes, but that's all right. I like music.'

'What do the voices say?'

'They tell me to go to church sometimes.'

'Do you go?'

'I used to, but the church is always closed so early in the morning.'

'How early?'

'About two or three o'clock. Then the voices stop, and I can't ask them what I should do next.'

'Do the voices stop any other time?'

'When I have a couple of drinks.'

'Is there anything else?'

'Just the bastard who walks beside me and whispers. I see his shadow, but every time I turn my head quickly he's moved. He's still just in the corner of my eye, but I've never been able to catch him.'

'Did it happen to you in jail?'

'Not after a few days. I felt safe. Nothing could reach me in jail'

'Mm.' He wrote in his file for a few minutes, and then handed me a green card. 'Now you don't have to go in the Army; you don't have to serve in the Armed Forces. You don't even have to go to the Labor Exchange if you can find a job without it. They cannot direct you to work anywhere you don't want to go. This is a Grade Four card.'

'What does that mean?'

'Your nerves are shattered, so you aren't fit for any service or any stress. If you are challenged by the military, the police, or any of the petty officials, you give them that card. It will show that you aren't a deserter, but that you aren't eligible for armed service. It should save you a lot of bother, so keep it with you. Try to be calm and don't get so angry.'

'Is that all?'

'I must send a report to your own doctor.'

'I've only seen a doctor once in my life. When I was nine, I had my appendix out.'

'I hope you feel better soon. Good luck.'

'Thank you.'

I sat on a wooden bench and looked at my card. All it said was 'Grade 4' and the date of the medical examination. It didn't seem a lot to show for five years service.

I was already twenty-two years old. I was dressed in stovepipe trousers, which made me look like a clown; I had no money and a sick mind. On the other hand, the war was over for me. My spirits brightened and I realized that a ton weight had lifted from my shoulders. I didn't feel so angry. I carried a passport to a new life in my hand—what a wonderful card. I'd get a job, some new clothes, and only drink beer. I could go on the open road; I was free to go anywhere I wanted.

I didn't know it announced to the world of officialdom that I was mentally unbalanced.

I sang as I went along the street. I wondered what excitement would happen next. I had no premonition of the sort of trouble that was in store for me. No one told me that sometimes the light at the end of the tunnel was an express train approaching. It seemed like a miracle when sanity was finally restored because it took ten years to happen. But that's another story.

The British Merchant Navy is in terminal decline. The Berlin Airlift, in 1948-1949 showed the ability of large aircraft to carry essential food to beleaguered cities. Technology brought Container ships that need few crew to service them. Many British ships and oil carriers are registered under Flags of Convenience; this is for several reasons. The Shipping Companies pay less in tax and much lower wages because they can sign on unskilled crew from Third World countries. They are non unionised, consequently safety goes by the board, as witnessed by constant oil spillages and other collisions and accidents.

It is a pity that the opportunities for boys from poor backgrounds to see the world and prove themselves men have disappeared. Some of my experiences were awful, but they WERE experiences and I wouldn't want to be without their memories.

Merchant Navy. R.I.P.

Epilogue

When I'd stowed away on my first ship I'd wanted adventure. I was penniless, but at seventeen it didn't matter. The Merchant Service certainly supplied the adventure, but I finished as poor as I had been five years earlier. My pay had started at around £9/2/6 a month, increasing to £13 when war came, and again to £18 by 1942; however, more than half that time I wasn't on a ship, so my total earnings for five years were only about £450. It's no wonder that £200 from the *Ironclad* seemed like the wealth of kings.

I came out with a lot of experience and appalling nightmares to last for the rest of my life.

In WW1 people like me were shot as cowards. In WW2 we were called bomb-happy and sent on our way. Now it is called Post Traumatic Stress Disorder. Subsequently, many years later, I was diagnosed as having PTSD, and granted a pension. It wasn't until 1974 that the Merchant Servicemen began to get pensions, but then only for wounds they could prove occurred in service.

Almost thirty years after the war ended. Better late than never – we were glad to receive it. Too bad for those who didn't last the distance.

When I walked away with my 'mad card,' as my friends called it, I was given no psychiatric treatment. I didn't notice this omission, as it never occurred to me that I had anything wrong with me. In hindsight, I consider myself very lucky to have avoided a frontal lobotomy, which left the patient just as crazy, but more amenable—quietly half-witted.

So time took its natural course and now I pass for normal, along with the millions of others who were war damaged, many of them much worse than I.

Just twenty-two years earlier in the First World War, I could have been shot for refusing to be drafted. Am I proud of my record? Of course not, but I didn't kill anyone.

Am I ashamed of my record? Most certainly not. I shoveled a hell of a lot of coal bringing food to Britain. Every merchant seaman did more to keep the country afloat than all the politicians put together.

The newspapers were constantly praising the Merchant Navy for their gallantry. 'How can we repay them?' they asked. Well, money would have been nice for a start. The service was treated appallingly. Not only was our pay stopped if the boat was sunk, but there was no sick allowance and no hospitalization. Wives and children got no pension—nothing except a telegram: **'We regret to inform you that your husband / son / brother is missing, presumed lost.'** I didn't have a financial stake or any future prospects to encourage my patriotism.

The fact that the King even thought that he wanted my services in the army to help him defend his seven or more castles, his horse drawn coaches, and the Crown jewels was puzzling. He'd had Churchill's 'two million soldiers bristling with arms' for years, and I was sure the millions of Americans would have given a hand. His situation must have been desperate, but I didn't want responsibility for his welfare. I was glad they'd had second thoughts about my usefulness to him and all his family.

After reading over these recollections, I wonder why I survived when 30,000 merchant seamen perished. At Tower Hill, near the Tower of London, there is a monument to those seamen who died in both World Wars. I often go into the Garden of Remembrance. The names of all the men are only carvings on stone now: there are not many left to mourn them.

I remember them, though. I can't forget them. Many were my shipmates.

THE END

Princess St, Jarrow after bombing.

The traitor William Joyce, known as Lord Haw Haw apologised for the bombing of this poor area. He said he would have dropped food parcels had he known it was Jarrow.

Unemployed. roam the streets. during the depression. 1932

FERRY BOAT LANDING, JARROW (294)

Jarrow to Howden ferry on which Sammy Cazeley served as engineer post-war.

Horses for all duties, fire engine, funerals and ambulance

Pat Shaughnessy left, Bill on right and father James Linskey .
Taken on return from Russia 1943

1941 Lisbon Portugal after 7 days in lifeboat. Young Harper on left, Bill in trilby hat and Canadian Williams.

MINISTRY OF TRANSPORT AND CIVIL AVIATION

G.R. 52

C.S.S./L.102/57/DC

Llantrisant Road,

2 Llandaff,

CARDIFF.

...........................195...

This is to Certify that.......William LINSKEY..................................who at the time of his engagement in the first ship named below gave the following personal particulars— ~~age~~ born 24.2.1921.............., nationality or birthplace.............Jarrow.......... appears by the Records in this Office to have served in the undermentioned ships in the capacities and during the periods stated.

Charles.

for *Registrar General.*

Ship's Name	Official Number	Port of Registry	Tons Gross	H.P.	Capacity in which he served	From	To	Trade*	Ability†	Conduct†
MARCONI	137532	Liverpool	–	–	Trimmer	1 Oct.1940	2 Jan.1941	F	VG	G
ASHBY	139249	West Hartlepool	–	–	Fireman Trimmer	15 Oct.1941	30 Nov.1941	F	VG	VG
*Vessel sunk by enemy action										
FLOWERGATE	143815	London	–	–	Fireman Trimmer	23 Jan.1942	22 May,1942	F	VG	VG
AMBERTON	149474	Newcastle	–	–	Fireman Trimmer	28 May,1942	27 Jul.1942	F	VG	D

* "F" Foreign; "H" Home; "C" Coasting; "Y" Yachting; "T" Fishing.
† "V.G." Very Good; "G" Good; "D" Declined; "N.S." Not Stated.

Fee :........................Four shillings and ....six pence.

(892)—868769/629/48—2M—2 57. P.F. 64-
